THE EXPERT WITNESS GUIDE FOR SCIENTISTS AND ENGINEERS

THE EXPERT WITNESS GUIDE FOR SCIENTISTS AND ENGINEERS

Alan E. Surosky

KRIEGER PUBLISHING COMPANY
MALABAR, FLORIDA
1993

Original Edition 1993

Printed and Published by
KRIEGER PUBLISHING COMPANY
KRIEGER DRIVE
MALABAR, FLORIDA 32950

Copyright © 1993 by Krieger Publishing Company

Library of Congress Cataloging-In-Publication Data

Surosky, Alan E.
    The expert witness guide for scientists and engineers / Alan E. Surosky.
        p.   cm.
    Includes bibliographical references.
    ISBN 0-89464-749-0
    1. Forensic engineering—United States.   2. Forensic sciences—United States.   3. Evidence, Expert—United States.   I. Title.
    KF8968.25.S87   1993
    347.73'67—dc20
    [347.30767]   92-25862
                                                                        CIP

10 9 8 7 6 5 4 3 2

CONTENTS

DEDICATION

To Nancy, my wife, who encouraged me to start this book, who inspired me to continue when my enthusiasm waned, and who motivated me to complete it at those times when encouragement and inspiration were not enough. Without her unwavering support this book would not have been written.

FOREWORD

Dr. Surosky writes the way he testifies. This guide for experts is simple, logical, and interesting. It is all relevant material for any scientist or engineer, lawyer, insurance adjuster, or frustrated juror.

This book provides the technical specialist with all of the information required to act as a forensic investigator and as an expert witness. It provides insight into the thinking of insurance companies, claims adjusters, and attorneys both for the defense and the plaintiff. It takes the reader through the investigation and litigation processes step by step. It describes the nature and techniques of friendly and hostile attorneys. It defines problems and pitfalls in communicating with lawyers, judges, and juries; and tells how to do it effectively. Finally, it shows the expert how to maintain a winning professional posture throughout a clearly adversarial process.

Technical experts can be divided into four categories: (1) always testify for plaintiff, (2) always testify for defendant, (3) testify for plaintiff or defendant, depending on who asks first, and (4) testify for plaintiff or defendant if convinced of correctness of position. Dr. Surosky is one of the extremely rare breed who fall into the last and best category.

I first saw him ten years ago when he was on the witness stand testifying against my client in a products liability case. His relaxed manner, clear explanations, and obvious integrity made his testimony compelling. After trial that day, I told my partner, "Well, he convinced me!" I need not tell you the outcome of that case, but we should have taken the defense's substantial settlement offer.

Dr. Surosky's integrity shows up at the front end of any case. Since that first meeting he has assisted us on a number of cases, but he has turned down many more of our cases than he has accepted. This manifest honesty and belief in any case he undertakes helped me in a case when Dr. Surosky had agreed to testify for our side. In closing argument defense counsel made the egregious error of suggesting Dr. Surosky might have manipulated the evidence. The jury would have none of that. They returned a substantial verdict for our client even though the defense had offered only a little more than nuisance value in a settlement offer.

As plaintiff's lawyers we think we only take good cases, but I am always more comfortable with a case when Dr. Surosky agrees with me on its technical merit. This book is "must" reading for anyone who wants to learn from one of the best.

Stephen J. Pajcic III
Attorney at Law
Jacksonville, Florida

PREFACE

I first testified as an expert witness some thirty-five years ago as the Engineering Manager of a major testing laboratory. The testimony concerned a product which the laboratory had evaluated, and which had become the subject of a civil dispute. While agreeing to testify as a job-related activity, appearance in court was not on any list of my professional goals or special skills.

The nature and the outcome of that case are forgotten. Well remembered are the apprehension at appearing in a strange forum, and the realization during cross-examination that I was an amateur facing a professional at his own game.

Since then, experience in myriad failure analyses, depositions, and court appearances has eliminated the apprehension, and probably has improved my effectiveness as an expert witness. While a technical expert is seldom the sole factor in winning or losing a case, the percentage of cases resolved satisfactorily for my clients has increased substantially in recent years.

If this can be attributed in part to improved performance, there exists this unfortunate corollary. During my earlier years at least some part of my on-the-job training was at client expense.

Most scientists and engineers qualify as technical experts early in their careers. This expertise normally increases both in quality and in scope with experience. Eventually the technical expert may become a "world class" specialist. Even this degree of professional skill is not enough to assure excellence as a witness.

The technical expert who would provide good expert testimony needs to learn the rules of the contest, some basic law, the effective use of forensic technology, what help is available, the tactics of the opposition, and finally the art of intellectual self defense.

Dealing with expert witnesses, both friendly and hostile, is a skill in which lawyers are well instructed as a part of their training. Dealing with lawyers, both friendly and hostile, is a skill in which most technical specialists are untutored.

This book tries to level the playing field in the technical expert and lawyer relationship. It is written in the hope that it may induce others to enter the domain of the expert witness, while avoiding most of the errors, pitfalls, and traps which are an inevitable part of the process of learning by experience.

Winter Springs, Florida
1993

CHAPTER 1

Introduction

"They cudden't get me into court as a witness; no, sir, not if't was to hang me best friend . . . I did it wanst; I'll do it no more."

—Finley Peter Dunne,
Mr Dooley on the Choice of Law

WHY TESTIFY

Any expert, unconcerned with and unprepared for the first hostile examination in a legal setting, may well experience the "Dooley" syndrome before it's over. Lacking information about the ways of the lawyers and the courts, that first experience can be traumatic. It doesn't have to be that way.

A healthy anxiety, inspiring solid preparation and mental alertness, can assure a creditable first effort as a technical expert in the seemingly arcane realm of civil litigation. An auspicious early experience can lead to career opportunities which are mentally stimulating, professionally satisfying, and financially rewarding.

Expert witness practice as a vocation or avocation requires a continuing effort to stay abreast of the latest technology in your area of specialization. It requires development of the ability to communicate clearly both with persons uninformed in your specialty, and with experts in fields where you have no expertise. It demands that you sharpen your ability to think rapidly under pressure. Finally, it dictates that you maintain the highest professional and ethical standards under what are usually highly adversarial conditions.

If you get the impression that this is a "high stress" activity, you make no mistake. But it is an increasingly important field of professional practice, and it does have its compensations.

You can help to assure fairness in the settlement of some of the many civil disputes which characterize our society. You can participate in procedures which aim at decreasing the perils of living in a high technology world. You can have the opportunity to enlighten others about the safety or dangers of those special factors of everyday life which are within the scope of your expertise. You can gain in professional prestige through public recognition of your expertise.

Most important, you can help fill an urgent need for professional technical services in a field where the financial impact on the litigants may be substantial; the importance of expert testimony is paramount; and the monetary compensation for the expert is commensurate with the challenge.

If the potential philosophical, professional, and financial satisfaction inherent in "expert testimony" practice outweigh your foreboding at working in an unfamiliar and often contentious environment, you meet the first requirement for a good expert witness.

CIVIL LITIGATION—A GROWING INDUSTRY

The business of litigation in the United States grew at a steady pace throughout this century. The growth accelerated in 1977 when the United States Supreme Court[35] ruled that advertising by law firms was constitutionally protected. A series of decisions during the following decade served to reinforce that right.

Some prophets of disaster felt the judicial and economic systems of the United States might collapse under an intolerable burden of liability laws, law suits, and irrational jury awards. Judge Richard Neely[28] said in 1988: "Data supporting the conclusion that liability law is going to become a more prominent hazard for the economy is all around us." Walter Olson[30] said in 1991: "America has deregulated the business of litigation. The experiment has been a disaster, an unmitigated failure."

The Supreme Court[36] currently holds an opposite view. Reaffirming its earlier positions, it decided in 1991 that punitive damages more than four times compensatory damages and two hundred times the actual expense of a plaintiff were constitutionally proper. Justice O'Connor, in a dissenting opinion, lent some credibility to the doomsday theorists.

She wrote: "Recent years . . . have witnessed an explosion in the frequency and size of punitive damage awards . . . It is now clear that the problems are getting worse, and that the time has come to address them squarely. The Court does address them today. In my view, however, it offers an incorrect answer."

The correctness of the decision may be debatable. The positive impact that it will have on increasing the future volume and economic impact of civil dispute resolution is not. Despite sporadic attempts to "reform" the legal process, the field will grow in magnitude for the foreseeable future.

WHO NEEDS AN EXPERT?

A better question in a complex and litigious society might be, who doesn't? The *Defense Counsel Journal*[34] spoke fairly for the legal community when it described the importance of the expert witness as follows. "In today's litigation, expert witnesses frequently determine the outcome of any given case. The influence they have on the outcome of any trial can never be overstated . . . All good trial lawyers are well aware of this and know that many trials become nothing more than a battle of experts."

The answer to the question, who needs an expert? clearly becomes either or both sides in any civil dispute. Government agencies involved in controversy with each other, or with their clients or contractors. Industrial or commercial organizations perceiving that a contract has been breached, or that their technology has been misappropriated unfairly. Individuals who have suffered physical or financial loss through what they consider negligence on the part of someone else.

In general, any individuals or groups who feel that they will be or have been damaged by what they consider to be the improper action of "others" are potential clients. So are the "others."

The opportunity for technical experts to participate at the earliest stage of the dispute process does occur, but it is rare. Most often the expert is not consulted until the possibility of significant financial gain or loss is clearly recognized. The predominant clients thus become insurance companies, claim adjustment companies, and lawyers for both the plaintiffs and the defendants.

The insurance and legal communities have the most structured requirements in the domain of civil dispute resolution. What follows is directed primarily toward these most complex operations in "expert witnessing." However, the expert witness skills applicable to this level of controversy are generally appropriate in any less demanding area of nonviolent dispute.

THE INSURANCE COMMUNITY

There are by recent count[2] more than twenty three hundred rated property and casualty insurance companies in the United States. These organizations differ in size from State Farm Insurance with over nine hundred claims offices and twenty two thousand claims employees to individually owned companies with one claim office and several claims employees.

Additionally, most major industrial organizations are either self-insurers, or carry insurance policies with very large deductible coverage. These organizations, through their risk management structure, assume the posture of an insurance company in the event of possible litigation. Regardless of size, the goals and methods of operation of these groups with respect to claims evaluation are remarkably similar.

Their primary goal is to remain profitable in a highly regulated environment. A dichotomy in public opinion sees insurers first as having almost limitless funds for claim payments, and second as having a primary responsibility for maintaining low premiums. The companies try to strike what they consider a proper balance between these factors through their claims evaluation structure.

Claims policy and overall responsibility lie with the main office, usually under the direction of a senior corporate officer with the assistance of in-house counsel. Activities involving the technical expert are usually initiated at the claims office level.

The local claims office typically is run by a claims manager. The manager may direct the activities of a number of claims supervisors and claims adjusters; or may wear all of those hats personally in a small office. Theoretically the function of the claims office is to settle all claims fairly and promptly. In practice the claims manager is usually under the pressure of continuing financial review as a measure of performance. Local claims personnel are thus strongly motivated to assure that claims are valid before payment.

Claims requiring skills beyond the expertise of claims office in-house personnel are legion. Electrical damage attributed to lightning; explosions or fires of unknown origin; automobiles that apparently move without operator input; structural failures; powered machines of all types that malfunction; sinkholes; environmental damage; construction hazards; alleged product design and manufacturing defects; hazardous chemicals; and so on. These types of claims are usually referred to outside technical experts for analysis.

The other major employer of expert services in the insurance community is the independent adjustment company. These, like the insurance companies, vary in size from the local one person operation to larger organizations with upward of five hundred claims offices.

The adjustment companies usually contract with insurance companies to furnish any services the insurance companies are not equipped to handle on a local basis. These vary from basic investigation and appraisal through complete handling of a claim, including negotiation and settlement. Like the insurance companies, the adjustment companies rely on outside experts for claims beyond their in-house skills.

Parenthetically, the insurance community is not always the defendant. Sometimes, because of legal intricacies, insurers partially or fully take the position of plaintiff.

THE LEGAL COMMUNITY

The legal community, for our purposes, consists of in-house counsel for the insurance or self-insuring companies, and trial attorneys for both the defense and the plaintiff. These are the shock troops of the litigation dispute. They have the greatest need for excellence in both technical and witness expertise. Thus, examination of their motivation and modus operandi is appropriate.

Our system of civil justice is based on the adversary principle. It assumes that if both parties to a dispute are able to argue their positions skillfully and forcefully in an impartial public forum, a proper and just solution will be found. It doesn't always work that way. Michael Cacace[7] points out that " . . . lawyers do the bidding of their clients in a system that, while attempting to protect the masses, sometimes rewards the few and the undeserving." Despite its flaws, the system is fairly effective, and it is the legal structure within which expert witnesses must function.

The lawyers are first and foremost advocates of the best interests of their clients. Their function is to advise on the intricacies of the law, the merits of the case, and the strength of the opposition. They then seek to arrive at a solution most favorable to the client and, if necessary, to argue in court only those facts which are favorable to the client's position. If this seems unfair, remember that the opposing counsel represents a countervailing force.

House counsel, defense attorneys, and plaintiff's attorneys all have this same primary motivation. Beyond that, their functions and operating methods diverge.

House counsel are usually employees of the insurer, and act as background players. They assist employers in evaluating cases, in selecting outside trial counsel, and in tracking the progress of the legal process. They usually perform an ongoing review of the legal documentation in order to update the company evaluation of its position. They sometimes observe courtroom progress from the audience to evaluate the impact of the evidence on the court. They may, from this position, be authorized to change settlement guidelines to try to avoid a jury decision. Or they may be allowed to reduce or withdraw a previous offer if they feel things are going well.

Trial counsel, both plaintiff and defense, function under economic pressures different from house counsel, and different from each other. While lawyers are professional practitioners, law firms are businesses. The law firm today operates in a competitive market, and has the expenses common to most other competitive business operations. Not the least of these are the costs of high technology access, e.g., computers, data base usage, and facsimile equipment; and the cost of business acquisition, e.g., marketing, sales, and advertising expense. The law firm that fails to operate according to sound business practice will ultimately fail to operate at all.

Defense counsel is usually retained by the party to a dispute with the proverbial "deep pockets." From this position they are effectively insulated from the peripheral pretrial and trial costs. Hence, they are more concerned with assembling the best team possible than they are with trial cost containment.

Due to the competitive pressures of client acquisition resulting from Supreme Court doctrine, plaintiff's counsel usually operates on a contingency fee basis. This means that pretrial and trial costs are borne entirely by the plaintiff's firm. Their position is described by the common trial firm television commercial theme, "no award, no cost." These firms are usually, but not always, more conservative with respect to incurring major costs for outside expert help.

THE ROLE OF THE TECHNICAL EXPERT

The technical expert can serve two primary functions in the technical investigation of a civil dispute: that of an investigating consultant, and that of a potential expert witness. The consultant role, usually required by the insurance community, differs substantially from that typically required by trial counsel. These differences often prevent the use of the original investigating expert as a trial witness.

Recall that insurers need enough information to permit a good evaluation of their exposure. This generally means written reporting of all the factors, both pro and con, that the expert finds in his analysis. If they have a problem, it is far better for them to know of it at once rather than to be surprised unpleasantly later. Your report may offer information and opinions that may be tentative, but which might prove harmful to your client in an adversarial proceeding.

The rules limiting the ability of the opposition to have access to your notes, reports, and thought processes are complex; and their ramifications will be explored later in some detail. It is sufficient to note here that usually (but not always) the work output of the consultant is protected from discovery by the opposition, while the efforts of the trial expert are subject to full disclosure.

Recall also that trial counsel is an advocate in an adversarial proceeding. The counsel presents evidence supporting only one side of a dispute. You can be certain that opposing counsel will supply all appropriate contrary information.

The technical expert is not an advocate for either side, but is ideally an unbiased witness whose professional opinion happens to concur with the position of the friendly counsel. The skills, relationships, ethical considerations, and techniques essential to this function are the subject of the rest of this book.

CHAPTER 2

The Essential Expert

"Risk and claim managers realize that winning or losing cases—in court or at the negotiation stage—often turns on a battle of the experts"

—Kevin M. Quinley,
Expert Witnesses: Eggheads on the Half-Shell

THE EXPERTS ARE SPECIAL

An expert according to Black[3] is "one who is knowledgeable in a specialized field, that knowledge being obtained from either education or personal experience." An expert witness is one "who has been qualified as an expert and who thereby will be allowed (through answers to questions posed) to assist the jury in understanding complicated and technical subjects not within the understanding of the average lay person."

Lay witnesses in court are legally limited as to what they can offer as evidence. They may testify only as to their personal knowledge of events involved in a dispute. What they think might have happened is not admissible. Any viewer of television legal fiction is familiar with the line, "Objection, that calls for an opinion (or conclusion) on the part of the witness." Expert witnesses are subject to no such limitation.

The rules governing expert testimony are not uniform in all jurisdictions, but in general they follow the Federal Rules of Evidence[11] 702, 703, and 704. Summarizing, they permit the expert witness to make inferences and develop opinions based on facts provided by others. They then allow the expert to enter these opinions into evidence, occasionally where the facts or data underlying the opinions are not admissible as evidence.

The courts tend to allow the expert witness considerable latitude in testimony, even where opinion borders on speculation. The other side of the coin is that the courts also allow opposing counsel considerable latitude in cross-examination in attempting to discredit that testimony.

An expert who acts in a professional manner, provides credible testimony, and who knows and observes courtroom protocol will usually be received respectfully by the court and treated as someone special.

THERE ARE EXPERTS AND THERE ARE EXPERTS

The technical skills needed for recognition by the courts as an expert are widespread in the scientific community. Most engineers and scientists working for industry or government qualify. Technical personnel employed by consulting firms, or self-employed as consultants are usually acceptable. So are most teachers of technical subjects in universities, colleges, and trade schools.

Different skills are required to be a good expert witness. The combination of good technical and good witness skills in one individual is relatively rare, a fact usually reflected in compensation.

Assuming technical competence, the primary requirement for the exemplary expert witness is the ability to communicate complex technical information to a jury of lay personnel in both a clear and a persuasive manner. The following characteristics help.

Be likeable. For judges and juries, this usually means be outgoing, but not overwhelming. Be confident, but not arrogant. Be courteous, but not obsequious. Be serious, but not grim. Be professional, but not pretentious. Show respect for everyone, including the opposition.

Be exciting. This means be animated. Talk with feeling. Don't be hyperactive. Don't be garrulous. Use positive body language. Keep explanations simple and clear without pontificating. Use interesting graphics and demonstrations. Remember that while testifying, the witness is being judged personally by the judge and jury. Hold the attention of the court by change of pace.

Be convincing. Be dignified. Be calm and composed. Highlight credentials with "street smart" narrative. Restrain displays of temper. Look the part. Show no bias. Don't be intimidated. Have a positive attitude. Know the subject better than anyone else in court. Have a firm and reasonable position. Defend your position with truth.

Exhibiting these characteristics is as much art as science, and thus difficult to quantify. I have never known anyone who is a perfect ten in all categories, but, with a little thought, most scientists and engineers should rate better than five in any of them. Specific ways to improve these ratings will be described in the discussion of depositions and trials.

There are three broad categories of technical expert witnesses: the in-house expert, the avocational expert, and the vocational expert. Each has advantages and disadvantages from the viewpoint of the trial attorney, and each can be sure that opposing counsel will point out the disadvantages to a jury.

Consider the case of an allegedly defective product. In theory, although not always in fact, in-house experts know the product better than anyone else, and thus should be in a position to defend its design and its quality. The primary disadvantage is that they are seen by the jury as employees of the defendant, and thus biased toward the product. They also suffer from the real disadvantage of lack of trial experience unless their employer is deluged with lawsuits.

The avocational expert will have some full or part time occupation other than that of accident investigation, failure analysis, or trial support activities. This includes academic, industrial, and business activities.

The advantage of avocational expert witnesses is that juries may perceive them as less biased than the other two types. Their disadvantage is that they don't know the product as well as the in-house expert, and they don't know the courtroom as well as the vocational expert. This type of expert witness is frequently used along with an in-house expert. If they are both effective, they can provide a formidable, but not impregnable, defense.

The last category is the full-time forensic expert. These people are technical experts who have become totally involved in litigation work by design, or as a result of success as an avocational expert. They may be independent consultants, or they may be employees of companies that specialize in providing expert support for the litigation market.

A number of such companies are identified in Appendix A. They provide training for their personnel through lectures, mock trials, cross-examination by panels of lawyers, research assistance, laboratory and model preparation, and pretrial testimony rehearsal. These companies tend to specialize in work for the insurance community since their efforts carry a price tag too high for most plaintiffs.

The disadvantage of full-time expert witnesses is that they may be perceived by juries as "hired guns"; "expert" experts whose services are for sale to the highest bidder. Their advantage is that, through experience, they develop the ability to find weak spots in an offense or defense. Also through experience, they develop the ability to present their findings in a clear and convincing manner to a jury.

Based on personal experience in each of these groupings, my own belief is that the effect of the witness category on credibility to a jury is more a matter of attorney perception than fact. Juries know, or they find out during a trial from opposing counsel, that all technical experts are paid substantial sums of money for their findings and testimony.

Juries seem to put this aside in their evaluation of expert testimony. No matter where the witnesses come from, if they score well on the criteria previously set out for the exemplary expert, the jury will like them, believe them, and give appropriate weight to their opinions.

CLIENT RELATIONSHIPS

The relationship between the lawyer and the technical expert is strange, and unlike any other the scientist/engineer is apt to encounter. Relating well demands that the expert fully understand the multiplicity of duties, the time constraints, the high stress, and the heavy responsibility under which the lawyer operates. Only through this understanding can the expert have a proper perspective regarding his own duties and functions.

Consider first that a trial attorney may be involved in several hundred cases at any one time. Many of these may be dropped or settled. Others will persist over a period of years to ultimate trial. New cases will continue to replace those that have disappeared. Thus, the lawyer in theory must be considering over a hundred intellectual problems at a time; a clearly impossible task for almost anyone.

As a result, most good trial lawyers have developed the ability to concentrate on the case at hand, blocking out of their minds most facts about other cases in their inventory. They also have developed the ability to quickly reassemble their thoughts regarding the next case when the last one is finished. This may sometimes frustrate the scientist/engineer.

Dedicated experts who wish to discuss some element of their own work with an attorney who is in the midst of a long hot trial on another matter may find their messages not read, and their calls not answered.

Experts are typically proud of their professional standing, and may consider this an insult. In fact it is probably no more than a reflection of lawyer concentration, and should be recognized as such.

Experts must realize that they are a small (albeit important) part of the team effort necessary to win one of many lawsuits in which their attorney client is involved. They can be assured that when their case reaches priority status, they will get all the attention they could hope for.

The lawyer is the manager, the coach and the key player on the litigation team. The function of the lawyer, simplified, is as follows. The plaintiff's attorney must establish that the client has been injured in an incident, that the injury is the fault of another party, that the other party was negligent in causing the injury, and that the client didn't contribute significantly to the injury through personal negligence. The extent and permanence of the injury, and the current value of the economic losses over the expected period of debilitation must be established. Finally the ability of the defendant to pay damages must be determined.

Thus the lawyer must deal at a minimum with lay witnesses, investigators, technical experts, medical experts, and economists in preparing a case.

Again simplifying, defense counsel in countering the plaintiff's attorney activities must establish a full team of investigators and experts to refute or minimize all of the plaintiff's allegations, and must develop a scenario in which his defendant client is blameless.

In both cases the primary role of the lawyers is as an advocate for their clients in a strictly adversarial procedure. The attorney's main goal is to win the case by any legal means. It is not their function or duty to seek a balanced verdict. It is their function and duty to do seek a resolution most favorable to their clients. While the success of a suit sometimes may hinge on a "battle of experts," there is little doubt that the suit itself is always a "war between lawyers."

This circumstance can conflict with the normal philosophy of a technical specialist. The usual approach to problem solving for the scientist or engineer is to review all available data, and then present both the pros and cons in justifying the selected solution. This approach is not practicable in an adversarial proceeding.

For any valid expert opinion on any subject, somewhere there is an expert or pseudo-expert ready to give a contrary opinion. The contrary view may come from an honest difference of opinion, or may come from a "hired gun" whose testimony is for sale to the highest bidder. A jury is usually capable of distinguishing the one from the other.

In any case attorneys are obligated to find experts who will support their side of a case. The techniques used by lawyers to explore the opinions of a technical expert with regard to a specific incident are varied. The boundary between ethical and unethical dealing between the lawyer and the technical expert constitute a gray area for the legal profession; one still in the process of being defined.

There are certainly logical areas of potential conflict between both the philosophy and the ethics appropriate to the two professions. These differences must be reconciled in the minds of the technical experts if they are to function effectively as expert witnesses.

PHILOSOPHY AND ETHICS

All of the scientific disciplines have a code of ethics promulgated by one or more relevant technical societies. These generally address two major areas of concern; the external interface aimed at protecting society, and the internal interface aimed at protecting the status quo.

Much of the code material was aimed at protecting established firms from competitive pressures such as advertising or competitive bidding. These areas of the codes have been invalidated for the most part by the Supreme Court, and are of no interest to us here. Our concern is with those areas of the codes dealing with professional ethics in the truly "ethical" sense; and with those peculiarities of "expert witnessing" which are not addressed by the codes.

Generally the "principled" sections of the various codes take the high moral ground. To act in an honorable and dignified manner. To be realistic and honest in testimony. To not misrepresent qualifications. To use professional skills in the best interest of public health and welfare. To act in accordance with high moral standards. To refrain from any act which would bring dishonor or discredit to the profession.

All of these are as hard to argue with as motherhood and apple pie, and it is assumed that these ideals are embraced by the reader. There are some witness-specific ethical and philosophical considerations which are not so clear cut.

Lawyers have a definite idea of what is needed from an expert to establish a case. They also know where they do not want the expert to go to avoid weakening the case. They will communicate this information to the expert in an unequivocal manner.

The expert is not an advocate, and will not usually go as far as the lawyer would like in providing testimony. What experts will say or will not say is a matter of their own priorities. Foremost among these must be maintaining the professional reputation and integrity which made them desirable expert witnesses in the first place.

The first rule of forensic work for the expert is be unbiased. Some bias does exist in the scientific community. Many technical specialists have established beliefs that corporations in general do their best to provide a safe high-quality product. They see any attack on any company as an attack on themselves. Other technical specialists have a strong bias toward the consumer, believing that corporations in general act purely for the generation of cash. Philosophically such experts would do well to avoid courtroom work, since a good attorney can usually expose such bias to the court in a manner certain to discredit testimony.

Second, do not offer yourself as an expert in areas where your expertise is marginal. Be sure your qualifications in the area in question can withstand close scrutiny. This means having solid training and experience which cannot be shaken by investigation or cross-examination. Feel free to search your background for appropriate experience, but be confident in your own mind that you are indeed expert in the area of dispute. You will certainly be tested in a controversial setting.

Third, avoid any conflict of interest. If you have had any significant discussion with one party to a dispute and rejected that person's position as untenable, refrain from acting as an expert for the opposing side for obvious reasons. As an independent expert, avoid cases in which you have a personal relationship with any of the parties to the dispute, or where you have a personal stake in the outcome. This, of course, precludes the expert witness ever working on a contingency basis where the fee depends on the outcome of the case.

Do not take a technical position in conflict with any previous stance you have taken, unless you are prepared to address the change in position and the reasons for it at the start of the proceedings. If there is some question in your mind whether you have a conflict of interest, the best course of action is to assume that you do. The loss of income is much less important than the possible loss of reputation.

Fourth, be certain the client is not trying to buy an opinion. Exploring the potential as an expert witness for their side of a case, attorneys have two good options. They can retain the expert as a consultant to review the case and determine the relative technical merits of each side of the dispute. If the findings are favorable, the expert can then be retained and identified as an expert witness.

Alternately, if they have sufficient information concerning all of the facts of the case, attorneys can state these facts in the form of a hypothetical question to ascertain the expert's probable opinion. (If you assume that all of these things I just told you are true, what would your opinion be as to the cause of the accident?). If retained, the expert would of course make his or her own investigation of the facts.

An unacceptable approach by an attorney is to define the testimony wanted from the expert without providing the opportunity for independent investigation. This arrangement is probably unethical for the attorney, is certainly unethical for the expert, and should be rejected out of hand.

Finally we are faced with the philosophical question, What is the truth? Jake Erlich,[9] the eminent trial attorney, wrote: "The man who speaks the truth may in fact say what is false, just as the man whose intent is to falsify may inadvertently speak the truth. Lying consists in saying the contrary of what one thinks or believes, and the withholding of truth is sometimes a worse deception than a direct lie."

The expert is sworn "to tell the truth, the whole truth, and nothing but the truth." There is, however, no obligation to provide answers to questions that have not been asked, or to lead the opposition into asking the "right" questions.

Assume that an imaginary corporation, the XYZ Manufacturing Co., has built and sold a machine called a model XYZ1000 Industrial Robot. Also assume the machine is less than one year old, has been operating for a total of six thousand hours without overhaul, and that a widget, a critical part of the machine, has failed due to abnormal wear causing a serious injury.

Further assume that the widget would not have failed if made from a commonly used stronger material. Finally assume that the manufacturer recommended a five thousand hour overhaul, during which the abnormal wear might have been found, and the widget replaced.

An expert called by the plaintiff can point out that the machine is fairly new, that the failed widget was the proximate cause of the accident, and that the widget material was not suitable for the application. If not asked the question, there is no obligation to render an opinion on the effect of failure to overhaul. Plaintiff's attorney certainly will not ask. If opposing counsel fails to ask on cross-examination, the subject may never come up. If the question is asked, the expert, of course, will express a truthful opinion.

Conversely, an expert called by the defense can point out that the failure to maintain the machine properly permitted the widget to operate beyond its intended life, and that its replacement would have prevented the accident. There is no obligation to render an opinion on the merits of the part design unless specifically asked by one attorney or the other. Again, the subject may never arise, but will be answered in accordance with the expert's honest opinion if the question is asked.

Questions by attorneys (restricted by the rules of evidence) thus develop those partial truths upon which juries must make critical decisions. The school of thought characterized by Erlich holds that suppressing part of the truth is effectively a means of lying. It assumes, probably correctly, that the more truth there is in an erroneous statement or opinion, the more difficult it is to reject.

The individual may have trouble in reconciling this situation with a sworn obligation to "tell the whole truth." In some cases the proper course of action is clear; in others there may be an ethical dilemma.

I can offer no general solutions to these problems. The philosophical and ethical considerations of each case differ. Personal conscience and thoughtful evaluation must be the final determinant in whether any given case warrants participation.

PICK YOUR CASES

The relationship between attorneys and technical experts is often tense because of their functional differences in the dispute, individual professional pride, disparity in goals, ethical differences, and the high emotional stresses imposed by the legal process.

Under the best conditions, forensic work is precise and demanding for the technical expert. There must be a comfortable feeling of mutual respect, integrity, and personality compatibility with the attorney. There must be confidence that no attempt will be made to manipulate the work of the expert. There must be assurance that enough time will be allowed for a full review of the matter in question. The expert must be sure of having adequate technical stature in the disputed area, and must be comfortable with the technical position assumed.

Unless you sense instinctively that all of these criteria are met, you are probably better off refusing the work. If you are careless in accepting assignments, you may be inviting some uncomfortable experiences. If you do pick your cases carefully, you will find most of the work gratifying and rewarding.

CHAPTER 3

Something About the Law

"It is likewise to be observed that this society (of lawyers) hath a peculiar chant and jargon of their own, that no other mortal can understand, and wherein all their laws are written . . . "

—Jonathan Swift,
Gulliver's Travels

YOU SHOULD KNOW THE LANGUAGE

Technical experts need not be proficient at law, but they should understand the significance of what they do and say during each step of litigation. They will seldom develop the skills needed to assist in the legal planning of trial strategy, but they should be able to help plan the presentation of technical evidence so that it is both informative and interesting to a jury. Finally, they must know enough about the law to grasp what the client attorney is telling them, and enough to avoid blunders which can dilute or destroy the effectiveness of their testimony.

This chapter does not intend to turn a technical expert into a lawyer, nor to allow debating matters of law safely with opposing counsel. I hope it provides enough information to make the litigation process less mysterious and less formidable. I also hope it will begin to make the expert aware of places along the way where traps and pitfalls may be set by opposing counsel.

ANATOMY OF A CIVIL DISPUTE

Most attorneys prefer negotiation to the uncertainties of trial. The litigation process terminates at any time with a settlement satisfactory to both parties. This usually occurs between the first notice of a claim and the time when the jury returns a verdict. Nevertheless, negotiation sometimes continues after the verdict, pending the appeal process, and may continue until the highest court having jurisdiction hands down a final decision.

The majority of cases involving expert testimony do not reach the trial stage. My own experience is that only about one case in five that passes the deposition stage will eventually reach the courtroom. Nonetheless, the cases reaching trial include the most controversial and the most economically significant. For this reason the Civil Dispute Process diagram (figure 1), and our discussion of its elements, include the complete scenario for those happenings in civil litigation in which the technical expert may be required to participate.

The terminology used here is essentially generic and applicable to most jurisdictions, but it is not universal. For example, a *complaint* in one court may be called a *claim, petition* or *declaration* in another. Where the terminology does differ, the meaning is easily recognized by context or semantic similarity.

The first element in a civil dispute is an *injury*, real or perceived. For our purposes injury may be defined as physical damage done to a person or property. The injured party may elect to pursue a claim outside the legal system through personal negotiation. Rarely will a technical expert be involved at this point. If negotiation fails and the claimant decides to pursue the matter further, a plaintiff's attorney is retained, usually on a contingent fee basis where payment depends on a successful outcome of the case.

Infrequently a plaintiff's attorney may have a case in which a plaintiff has the personal determination and means to pursue a claim on a fee-paid basis as a matter of policy, even where the possible economic redress does not warrant the action. More often, prior to accepting a case, the plaintiff's attorney will evaluate the case on the basis of its potential contingency value.

The criteria for acceptance are usually injury severe enough to warrant significant financial redress, the probability of identifying and securing a judgment against legally responsible defendants, and the ability of the defendants to pay an awarded judgment.

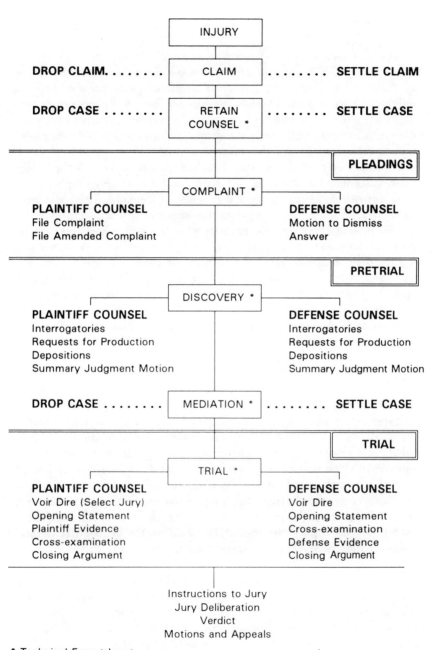

* Technical Expert Input

FIGURE 1 The civil dispute process

The decision to accept or reject is not trivial because plaintiff's counsel normally underwrites litigation expense. In major cases the dollar cost may be well into six figures, a substantial loss for the attorney unless the case is won. The first assignment for a technical expert may occur here as a consultant in case evaluation. Having accepted the case, plaintiff's attorney will notify the defendant or defendants of the intention to seek damages for the injury.

Plaintiff's counsel makes the client's demands known to the defendant, describing the basis for the claim, and the redress sought. Some firms provide a settlement brochure with the demand. This document summarizes the case by providing among other things, witness statements, investigation reports, photographs, medical reports, expert reports, and the extent of the damage. At this point the defendants will involve their in-house claims department, or their insurer.

Technical experts again may have input by providing the adversaries with the scientific validity of their respective positions. Assuming that a negotiated settlement is not reached, plaintiff's counsel files a complaint with a court supposedly having jurisdiction. Thus starts the *pleading* phase of the litigation process.

Pleadings

Expert input in wording a complaint can make the complaint stronger technically, and can preclude the need to amend the complaint during subsequent proceedings. Appendix E displays a typical complaint format.

Plaintiff's counsel will seek to file the complaint in a court, state or federal, where the local rules and timing are most favorable to the client position. Later, the defense will try to move the case to a jurisdiction where the rules are more favorable to the defendant. The technical expert has no input, but should be made aware by counsel of any idiosyncrasies with regard to expert testimony in the jurisdiction selected.

The defendants, having sufficient financial resources to meet the case acceptance criteria, will now retain defense counsel. Where there are multiple defendants, there may be more than one defense firm involved. Because defense attorneys usually work on an hourly fee basis, acceptance of the case for the defense tends to be routine.

There is some economic incentive here for defense counsel to avoid an early negotiated settlement unless pressured to settle by the client.

Also, defense counsel is generally less concerned than plaintiff's counsel about the cost of retaining technical expert assistance, since the defense expense is reimbursed regardless of the outcome.

Once the complaint is filed, legal activities begin. The defendants must file an *answer*. This may take a number of forms. A *denial* that the defendant is liable based on the alleged facts. An *affirmative defense* based on new facts. An *equitable* defense based on justice or fairness. A *counterclaim* that the plaintiff is liable to the defendant. Or a *cross-claim* where one of multiple defendants blames another. In case of a counterclaim, plaintiff's counsel files a *reply*, a defensive pleading responding to the new allegations.

The contents of all of these documents should be examined carefully by experts on both sides of the suit, since they often contain pertinent technical information.

The defendant(s) also may file a *third party complaint* against someone not a party to the original suit, alleging the fault was that of the third party. The original defendant now also becomes the third party plaintiff. The third party defendant may file a *fourth party complaint* against someone else, and so on ad infinitum.

In practice, multiparty suits are unusual but interesting. Attorneys and experts for the defendants frequently argue among themselves, each pointing out the weak points in the other defenses. This tends to make life easier for the plaintiff's attorneys, and more complicated for the defense. The experts on both sides have a more complex task since they will be examined by multiple attorneys with differing concerns.

Pretrial

This stage of the process is where most of the expert effort will be expended, and where the maximum technical impact on the outcome of the case will be developed.

Pretrial activities start with *discovery*. The rules of discovery in civil cases are much more liberal than in criminal cases where the constitutional protection against self-incrimination exists. The discovery elements which most affect the work of the expert are *interrogatories*, *requests for production*, and *depositions*.

In theory, these procedures permit each party access to most of the information concerning the case which is in the possession of the opponent. In fact, the sharing of this information is less than perfect. Some information is not legally discoverable, some is withheld by legal maneuvering, and some, regrettably, is withheld by misrepresentation.

The work product of the attorney in developing a suit is not discoverable, being classed as *privileged*. Attorney communication with a technical expert whose role is that of consultant, and not trial witness, is usually protected by this privilege. However, since the consultant may end up being a witness at trial, it is safer to assume from the start that all expert communication eventually will be discovered.

In the ideal situation, prior to, or early in the discovery process, the expert will have had the opportunity to examine all the documents and physical evidence available. Some information, such as other expert opinion, may be withheld from the expert at this time by the client attorney in order to insure an unbiased opinion, and to keep open various options.

The expert should have made an initial on-site investigation, developed a preliminary opinion as to a probable scenario, and should have a feeling for what further information is needed to support or disprove the theory. These actions require that the expert be retained early in the legal process, a prerequisite frequently not met.

Now start the interrogatories. These are a series of written questions served by each adversary on the other. They must be answered in writing under oath, thus clarifying the positions of the opponents. Interrogatories may ask about other similar injuries or lawsuits, quality control and fabrication procedures, engineering responsibility, insurance coverage, corporate organization, and a multitude of other matters. A typical interrogatory (with answers) including expert witness inquiries is shown in Appendix E. The expert, of necessity, will assist the attorney both in framing questions for the opposition, and in answering questions from the opposition.

Production, usually occurring in the same time frame as the interrogatories, is initiated by a *request for production* or *notice to produce*. It is a request to examine tangible evidence controlled by the opponents. This includes, among other things, hardware examination, accident site inspection with photography and measurements permitted, and copying of drawings and documents. Appendix E includes a typical production request format.

In the event of reluctance of either party to agree to the production request, the court will establish ground rules for production in response to a *motion to compel discovery* or *motion for a protective order*. The primary role of the expert in the production process is the identification and description of the things needed for examination in order to develop a valid final opinion.

The element of discovery most affecting the expert is the deposition. This process permits the opposing attorney to question the witness under oath, the testimony being recorded and transcribed by a court certified reporter. The deposition is, in a sense, a fishing expedition with a fairly wide scope. Its purpose is to evaluate the apparent credibility and behavior of the opposing expert witness under stress, to determine the opinions of the expert, and to fix those opinions pending trial.

The witness may be asked to appear at the deposition location informally, or may be ordered to appear by a *subpoena*, or *subpoena duces tecum*. The subpoena, from the Latin "under penalty," is a court order to appear. The subpoena duces tecum, "under penalty bring it with you," is an order to appear, usually with everything used in developing an opinion. A typical subpoena duces tecum is shown in Appendix E.

The deposition, to some extent, allows opposing counsel to develop trial strategy that will attack any personal or technical weaknesses exhibited by the witness. This is the first adversarial lawyer "game" to which the witness is exposed on a person to person basis. Good technique by the expert witness minimizes any potential advantage to the opposing counsel.

Other components of the pretrial stage do not involve the expert except in the occasional filing of an *affidavit*, a written statement under oath, to support or oppose a motion for summary judgment. Pretrial activities allow the attorneys to reevaluate their cases, and offer another chance for a negotiation. If none of the motions are granted, and if negotiation is unsuccessful, either party can ask that the suit be put on the court calendar for trial.

The final step of the pretrial phase may be a settlement or mediation conference. This can consist of an informal meeting between opposing attorneys, meeting with an uninvolved attorney (or attorneys) acting as mediator, or a formal hearing before a judge. The mediator or judge may suggest, but cannot force, a settlement. The suggested settlement permits the attorneys to get a feeling for their relative strengths and weaknesses as perceived by a knowledgeable third party, as well as the probable financial value of the claim. If mediation fails, the trial phase begins.

Trial

The first order of business is jury selection, a process called *voir dire*. Defined by legal dictionaries as "to speak the truth," the literal translation from the French is "to see to say." It is in fact an adult version of "show and tell" for prospective jurors. This permits attorneys to question and evaluate jury candidates with a view for acceptance or rejection within certain legal limits.

Expert input to voir dire lies first in suggesting to counsel technically oriented questions for prospective jurors. If qualified by experience, the expert may also suggest the types of jurors most likely to understand and evaluate fairly the technical theories involved, and the types most likely to prejudge or reject them.

Prospective jurors have seen television crime dramas where the *burden of proof* for the prosecution is *beyond a reasonable doubt*. This is a judgment call for the jury, but generally requires better than a 90 percent probability for any single piece of evidence to be persuasive. Most jurors expect the plaintiff to meet this standard in a civil case unless instructed otherwise. During voir dire, the plaintiff's attorney probably will stress that this is not the level of evidence necessary for a positive verdict in a civil trial.

The burden of proof in a civil suit is a *preponderance (or greater weight) of the evidence*. This means simply that the jury must find the plaintiff's allegations more probable than not, 51 percent probability being enough. Thus, the opinions of experts in criminal trials must be developed with *scientific certainty*, in civil trials with *scientific probability*.

A third standard of proof, *clear and convincing* evidence, lies somewhere between reasonable doubt and preponderance of the evidence. It controls punitive damages in some jurisdictions, and is probably the minimum personal goal that an expert should set in developing opinions.

Next the plaintiff's attorney makes an *opening statement* explaining what the suit is about, and outlining to the jury the evidence they will hear and see, together with its significance. While the opening statement is not supposed to include argument, the jury is assured that they will find for the plaintiff once the evidence is presented. Then defense counsel addresses the jury with a contrary view of what the evidence means, and assures the jury that by any reasonable interpretation they will find for the plaintiff. The trial has now begun.

Plaintiff's attorney has the burden of proof, and thus presents the plaintiff side of the case first. The basis for the suit is established normally by calling as initial witnesses the plaintiff, lay witnesses, and then the technical experts whose function is to establish *liability*.

The expert undergoes *direct examination* by retaining counsel, followed by *cross-examination* by opposing counsel. There may follow *redirect examination* to counter cross-examination, and *recross-examination* to counter redirect. If the witness does a creditable job, there is usually very little redirect and no recross-examination.

After following this process with the examination and cross-examination of medical and economic experts, the plaintiff's counsel rests.

Defense counsel follows the same routine with defense witnesses. The primary function of the defense experts is to refute the alleged liability claims. Subject to the same examination as the plaintiff's technical experts, their relative credibility plays a major role in helping the jury determine the technical truth. Medical and economic experts now testify for the defense. Then the defense rests.

Plaintiff's counsel may now present new evidence and previously unidentified experts in *rebuttal* of the evidence submitted by defense counsel. Defense counsel is then entitled to the *surrebuttal* presentation of new evidence and witnesses to respond to the new evidence by the plaintiff. Now the technical experts can rest.

Plaintiff's counsel presents *closing arguments* to the jury, summarizing all the positive aspects of the evidence. Defense counsel presents closing arguments with a contrary interpretation of the evidence. Plaintiff's counsel sometimes speaks in final rebuttal, and the judge instructs the jury regarding the facts and the law. The jury retires to its deliberations to consider liability and, finding liability, to assess damages.

The legal process may continue with motions for judgment notwithstanding the verdict, motions for new trials, and appeals. Technical experts play no role in these proceedings, their potential input having ended just prior to the closing arguments.

TORT LAW

A *tort* is defined as a private or civil act, wrongful under law, which causes injury to someone's person, property, reputation, or feelings. Excluded are *breach of contract or trust*, except where *bad faith* is involved. Embraced are a profusion of acts including, but not limited to, *assault, infliction of emotional distress, trespass, libel, malpractice, false imprisonment, fraud,* and *negligence.* Tort law allows the injured party to seek damages, usually monetary, in civil court.

The most common basis for a tort lawsuit is negligence. Negligence is defined, somewhat less than precisely, as the failure to exercise the care of a reasonably prudent person in a given situation. Negligence may be active or passive; either doing what should not be done, or not doing what should be. The finding of negligence in most cases is arguable because of its loose definition. That's what keeps the judges and juries busy.

Judgment for the plaintiff requires proof of liability on the part of the defendant. Liability generally requires a showing of either negligence or intent in causing an injury. There are a number of valid defenses to these allegations, including, among others, self-defense and contributory negligence. The reader interested in a clear and detailed explanation of the rules and defenses in tort litigation is referred to the text by E. J. Kionka,[22] *Torts.*

Involvement of the scientist/engineer with non-product-oriented tort cases usually consists of accident reconstruction followed by technical analysis. These investigations tend to address the actions of people in the application of technology, rather than flaws in the technology itself.

An automobile accident caused by failure to observe traffic signals is a general tort case. The same accident caused by brake failure may become a *product liability* case. In the case of multiple defendants, the allegations may be both negligence by the seller, and negligence and/or defective product by the manufacturer.

The predominant subset of tort litigation involving the technical expert as a witness is that of product liability. This may be attributed partly to the liberal interpretation of liability laws as applied to manufacturers, and partly to their ability to pay substantial judgments.

PRODUCT LIABILITY

The concept of product liability holds both the manufacturer and the seller of a defective product responsible for injury caused to buyers, users, or bystanders because of the defect. Under some conditions the defendants may be held to the rule of *strict liability*, or liability in the absence of negligence.

A product defect is one that makes it unreasonably dangerous for the user, or dangerous to an extent beyond what an ordinary user might contemplate. The basis for product liability is usually defective design, defective manufacture, or failure to warn of the hazards of an inherently dangerous product. Where the doctrine of strict liability is invoked in a complaint, it is common to include a coinciding allegation of negligence if it can be supported.

The principal defense against a product liability claim is that the product was not defective when it left the defendant's hands. Other defenses include claims that the product is state of the art, alternate designs would have an unreasonable impact on product cost and performance, the product is equal or superior to other competitive products, and the product was improperly altered or used.

The reader interested in exploring the technical aspects of these matters further is directed to Weinstein et al.,[39] *Products Liability and the Reasonably Safe Product*, to J. Kolb,[23] *Product Safety and Liability*, and to C. Witherell,[43] *How to Avoid Product Liability Lawsuits and Damages*.

MISCELLANY

Other legal factors affecting the attorney's evaluation of a suit are those of *contributory negligence, comparative negligence*, and the consequences of Workers' Compensation Acts.

Contributory negligence is the failure on the part of the injured party to exercise ordinary care in self-protection, where such carelessness (along with any negligence by the defendant) is a direct cause of the injury. In common law contributory negligence usually prevents recovery from the defendant. Most jurisdictions have now adopted the more liberal concept of comparative negligence.

Comparative negligence is a percentage measurement of the relative contribution of the plaintiff and defendant in causing the injury. Any damage award is reduced by the percentage of negligence attributed by the jury to the plaintiff. A judgment for the plaintiff including comparative negligence usually requires that the fault of the plaintiff is less than that of the defendant, and that, in many jurisdictions, the plaintiff with ordinary care could not have avoided the effects of the defendant's negligence once it was apparent.

Most workers are insured for injury in the workplace under Workers' Compensation Acts. These establish strict employer liability for accidents and diseases arising from employment. Thus, the employee need not bring legal action to establish negligence on the part of the employer in order to be compensated. The amount and duration of compensation are defined by the various laws.

The flip side of the coin is that employer liability is limited to the compensation provided by the laws, and further recourse against the employer is barred except where *gross negligence* is involved. Expert participation in industrial accidents is thus limited typically to those incidents in which the supplier of the equipment involved can be sued for providing a defective product; or those in which subcontractor personnel are injured by, or cause injury to, contractor personnel.

The technical expert who strives for excellence as a consultant or expert witness in the legal arena must always remember the function of the lawyers, and the constraints of the laws. The reader by now should have a feel for what legal guidance to seek from the client attorney prior to undertaking a technical investigation.

CHAPTER 4

Case Investigation

"I keep six honest serving-men; (they taught me all I knew)—Their names are What and Why and When—And How and Where and Who"

—Rudyard Kipling,
The Elephant's Child

LOOKING FOR HOW AND WHY

Forensic investigation is simple in theory. All you need are the "six honest serving-men." In practice, it is complicated by a lack of information and by misinformation, both inadvertent and deliberate.

Accidents requiring technical investigation are usually documented well and early. What happened, where it happened, when it happened, and who was involved in any injury are all matters of fairly accurate record at the time a technical expert is introduced to a case. How and why it apparently happened is usually a blend of fact and fancy that tends to vary with the storyteller. The probability of how and why it really happened is in the domain of expert opinion.

STANDARD INVESTIGATION METHODS

There are some standardized investigation procedures useful where incidents are subject to frequent occurrence, for example fires or automobile accidents. There are also some formal techniques for general accident investigation which result in producing data beyond that which is ordinarily needed by an expert witness.

Procedures for fire investigation are standardized by the U.S. Bureau of Alcohol, Tobacco, and Firearms.[38] SAE (Society of Automotive Engineers) publishes, and updates annually, collections of articles covering automobile accident investigation and reconstruction. Suggested SAE readings are *Accident Reconstruction, State of the Art,*[32] and *Motor Vehicle Accident Reconstruction: Review and Update.*[33]

The formal analytical procedures for general investigation are used mainly for inquiries outside the legal arena, where the primary goal is the avoidance of future similar occurrences. Thus, they are oriented toward providing "lessons learned" information to management, both in government and industry. They are predominately effective for team investigation of major accidents such as aircraft crashes, plant explosions, or the collapse of large structures.

Generalized accident investigation procedures include, among others, MORT (Management Oversight and Risk Tree) and STEP (Sequentially Timed Events Plotting) techniques. These are overly complex for basic accident investigation. They may be worth reviewing as an intellectual exercise by the technical expert, because they present methodologies for thinking in terms of logically sequenced investigation.

The Management Oversight and Risk Tree (MORT) technique was conceived by the National Transportation Safety Board, and adopted by the Atomic Energy Commission, now the U.S. Department of Energy. Essentially an accident prevention and control system, details of its application are presented in two publications by its principal developer, William G. Johnson: *Accident/Incident Investigation Manual,*[20] and *MORT Safety Assurance Systems.*[19]

The Sequentially Timed Events Plotting (STEP) technique was developed by Hendrick and Benner, and its methods are detailed in the text *Investigating Accidents With STEP.*[17] The approach is a second generation development of MORT technology with emphasis on graphic and systematic data collection. Primarily a tool for educating management through the "back to the drawing board" process after a mishap, it does provide some insight into methodical accident investigation.

A useful procedural document for the technical expert new to accident investigation is the work by Ferry, *Modern Accident Investigation and Analysis.*[12] Like MORT and STEP, this book views accident investigation mainly as a means to generate management action through the "lessons learned" process. Ferry, however, does a credible job of making a science of the art of accident investigation. While much of this text is classroom oriented, a number of real life incident scenarios and possible causes are presented.

Any of these documents can provide a line of departure for undertaking an accident investigation as a potential expert witness. None of them should be followed rigorously because they all view accident investigation as a learning process rather than the start of an adversarial procedure. Remember that your investigation will often start where others using the described techniques have ended, and the results of their investigations should be available to you.

In the final analysis, if you have common sense and are skilled at what you do, you should have no problem determining the most probable cause of any accident involving your area of expertise.

I HAVE A CASE

An invitation to the world of the forensic expert usually comes in the form of a telephone call or letter from an attorney because of a referral, your personal efforts to develop this type of practice, or your employment by a company with a plaintiff or defendant relationship.

The basic message is "I have a case involving a model XYZ1000 Industrial Robot, and would like to talk about the possibility of your acting as a consultant to me in this matter." Ideally, and for the purposes of this chapter, the call comes before the filing of a complaint rather than in a moment of panic just before the end of the discovery process.

Whether accepting the assignment or not, the time for taking notes and starting a case file is the time of the initial contact. You may decline a case for any number of reasons. Later, called on and wishing to work for the opposition, notes of your discussion with the first caller are essential in evaluating your ethical and legal position.

A primary attribute of any good lawyer is the ability to distort the meaning of hostile testimony. Written notes can offer opposing counsel avenues for attacking your credibility. Without proper care, the potential for subsequent problems starts with the first note taken. Record keeping for legal use differs from that for other technical purposes. Remember that notes, and not just final reports, may be subject to subsequent rigorous adversarial review.

KEEP A LOG, NOT A DIARY

The most probable scenario for any incident gradually develops with the acquisition of evidence, the passage of time, and the consideration of all reasonable possibilities. There are some interim ideas which you will reject summarily, and others which will be rejected after some considerable thought. Don't write any more than is necessary before your final opinion is fixed. Gratuitous notes are an invitation to opposing counsel to misrepresent your thought processes while deposing or cross-examining you.

You may safely record without comment any factual data concerning what, when, where, and who. Your initial opinions as to why and how should be discussed only orally, and only with the client. They should be identified as tentative, and associated with what investigative tasks will be required to confirm or deny their probability. An appropriate contact memo format for starting a case file for legal purposes is shown in the Contact Memorandum, Figure 2, Appendix C. Initial notes should be no more specific than shown in this example.

As the investigation progresses the amount of information to be retained and considered will increase geometrically, some cases developing thousands of pages of testimony and supporting exhibits during the typical one or two year period between the initial contact and the trial. Written notes and summaries become a necessity except for someone with an extraordinary memory.

Here again, use personal shorthand techniques and mnemonics to keep the notes from guiding opposing counsel into areas which can serve to obscure your opinions. Don't make notations on copies of documentary evidence you receive. Rather keep a separate log of memory joggers for all items you consider important in a document, along with their location in the document.

In legal transcripts each page and line is numbered. Notation of page and line number on the log sheet is usually enough to bring you back to those items of testimony which may be important in developing an opinion. If you are concerned with forgetting the reasons for the notation, a noncommittal word or two should be enough to help reclaim the thought later.

Summarizing, keep a full and accurate factual log of dates, times, people, places, physical observations, and measurements. Until your thoughts and opinions are final, keep them in an abbreviated form that only you can decipher. My own preference is to keep all case notes in a computer file which can be updated continuously so that the information is complete, contemporary, and free of ambiguity.

FOLLOW THE PAPER TRAIL

The documents available when first undertaking a case frequently contain enough "how and why" information to permit developing a probable preliminary scenario. Examine these records carefully, but take them all with a grain of salt.

Discrepancies almost always exist in witness statements, postaccident reports, equipment manuals, maintenance records, and other associated material. More than any other single factor, early perception of these discrepancies by the expert permits productive on-site investigation with the recognition of elements that eventually may be the crux of dispute.

The injured party, if not deceased, tends to remember things after an accident that may be at odds with some of the evidence. For example, a subsequent written statement may indicate that all reasonable precautions were taken. This loses some credibility if the plaintiff said while being rescued, "That was a stupid thing for me to do." I have known remarks of this type to weaken cases, but not necessarily destroy them. It is within the area of expert analysis to determine if it was indeed a stupid thing to do, or alternately if it was a foreseeable error that a reasonable person might be expected to make on occasion.

Statements of other involved witnesses tend to be self-serving. For instance, a service manager who says "I examined the XYZ1000 immediately after the accident and it worked perfectly; and it has always been maintained exactly as the manufacturer recommended" has a personal interest in the acceptance of that statement. Note the assertion, but be sure at a later date to check procurement and service records, talk with the service mechanics in private, and examine the XYZ1000 carefully if permitted to do so. If not permitted, the verification desired becomes a proper subject for the discovery process that will ensue.

Statements by noninvolved witnesses also tend to be shaded by personal bias and to conflict in matters of fact. News accounts of aircraft accidents often cite some witnesses who saw a mid-air explosion followed by a flaming descent, and others who saw the same aircraft hit the ground and then burst into flames. Again, note all witness statements, but seek independent verification.

Accident reports by plant safety officers, medical personnel, Occupational Safety and Health Administration (OSHA) inspectors, police, coroners, and insurance adjusters provide useful factual information. Here too, however, the facts may be obscured by personal observations which are at odds with expert theory. If you have good reason to think some of this material is in error, don't hesitate to take issue with it.

In rebuttal, however, don't dispute any evidence unless it directly impairs your theory of the most probable scenario. The more you can accept of the evidence as it exists, the less effort will be needed to convince a jury that you are right and that other evidence is in error. Countering opposition expert testimony is hard enough. If possible, let the rest of the evidence support your position.

CASE REVIEW

Having examined the documentation carefully, and assuming you have not yet met with the client attorney, next on the agenda should be an in-depth case review conference. This can be done by telephone, but a face-to-face meeting is preferable. It provides both the opportunity for mutual evaluation, and a chance to make a "stop or go" decision based on the needs of the client and the preliminary hypothesis of the expert.

If the case appears to have merit, and there is a mutual feeling of confidence between the expert and the client, the next essential is a site inspection if site events are germane to the opinion. Failure to visit an accident site can be used by opposing counsel to cast doubt on expert credibility if the expert opinion is in any way based on what happened at the scene.

If your testimony applies only to the design of the failed widget in the XYZ1000 Robot, you may get away without visiting Anytown Steel Company. If you are to testify whether or not the widget caused the accident, a plant visit is essential.

Now is the time to get a feeling from the client for the amount of cooperation you can expect during different phases of the investigation. If your client represents the defendant, you can usually be sure of ready access to design and manufacturing data, a supply of test parts, and exemplar machines where applicable. If employed by the plaintiff, you may need all the power of the courts in support of the discovery process to get a limited part of the needed information.

Cooperation at the site of an industrial accident is a mixed bag. Industrial organizations are sympathetic to the problems of their suppliers, and tend to view plaintiff's experts with alarm. On the other hand, recovery of damages by a plaintiff ordinarily results in some refund to workers' compensation underwriters, and thus has a beneficial effect on employer insurance premiums. Work site attitudes vary from completely defensive to fully cooperative.

The nature of this support will determine how the site visit should be handled. If you anticipate a poor reception, you should make a full-scale investigation on your first visit. It may be the only chance you'll have. If you expect a good relationship with accident-site personnel, it is easier and more effective to make a preliminary inspection in anticipation of another more definitive visit at a later date.

The same considerations apply to physical evidence. If it is in the possession of your client, you will be able to examine it as often as you wish. If it is in the possession of the opposition, your access will be limited, and the time for test and evaluation may be severely restricted.

Taking the conservative view that limited cooperation will be available at the site of the accident, careful preparation for any visit is warranted. Note all of the "what, where, when and who" information that you want to verify. Note all of the site information you will need to support or alter your preliminary deductions. Identify the measurements you will need, and the tools and instruments necessary to make them. Do a preliminary literature survey sufficient to refresh your memory as to industry practice and accepted standards.

The Site Survey Agenda, Figure 3, Appendix C, is a suitable note format in anticipation of most site surveys. The form can be modified to fit special conditions and personal preferences. Once again the content may be subject to discovery, and the notes should be noncommittal.

HANDLING TANGIBLE EVIDENCE

The evidence which forms the basis for expert opinion is of two types, tangible and testimonial. Tangible evidence, also called real or demonstrative, is evidence that directly addresses the senses of the observer without intervening testimony. It includes among other things documents, models, photographs, exhibits, and equipment or parts whose failure is alleged to be the proximate cause of an accident. This last category is critical in any lawsuit, and requires special handling.

Someone will have control of such evidence after an accident, and its subsequent location and control until it appears at a trial is subject to establishing a *chain of custody*. The location and control of the XYZ1000 Robot will probably not change. The allegedly defective widget may pass through many hands both plaintiff and defense.

The receipt and disposition of the widget should be carefully documented, the widget should be identified by nondestructive markings and photographs, and should be kept in a safe place by the custodian. A suitable Evidence Custody form is shown in Figure 5, Appendix C.

You should not examine or test the evidence in any way that would alter it significantly without permission of the opposition. If destructive testing is necessary, it may be negotiated by the attorneys, compelled by the court, or not allowed. If destructive testing is permitted, the opposition experts will probably be present to witness the procedure. If not allowed, you will have to find an alternative approach.

Critical tangible evidence may be the vital link in winning or losing a case. Loss or destruction can create a financial liability for the custodian. Treat it accordingly when it is in your possession.

SITE SURVEY

The investigation of an incident requires caution and prudence on the part of the expert to avoid needlessly arming the opposition. While determining the how and why, remember that your goal is to acquire evidence, not to dispense it. Ask probative questions; avoid answering them if you can. If courtesy requires answers, "I don't know about that" or "I'll have to think about that" are useful responses.

As in document analysis, keep your interim thoughts and opinions to yourself, and your notes cryptic. Use photography and videotape to record the information you need. Photos and tapes should permit you to reconstruct your memory of the site at a time when you can think without distraction and make notes that can withstand opposition scrutiny.

No matter how careful you are, almost inevitably you will find later that you missed a measurement or data item available only at the site. If you are fortunate you will be able to revisit; if not, you will have to make do with what you have. Film and videotape are relatively cheap. Use them generously, and they may help you remedy your omissions.

An appropriate note format for a site survey is shown in Figure 4, Appendix C. More definitive information should be in the form of physical measurements, abbreviated cryptic notes, videotapes, and photographs.

THE COMPLAINT

Once an expert for the plaintiff has developed various tentative scenarios based on prediscovery information, the complaint should be worded to include all of those factors essential to these scenarios. In the event a complaint has been filed prior to this time, an amended complaint (or second, third, or more amended complaints) can be filed if they are timely with regard to the jurisdictional process.

While including specific allegations supporting the expert's preliminary opinions, the causes of action listed should be extensive. The complaint should describe the alleged nature of the deficiencies, without directly suggesting means of either correcting them or avoiding resulting injuries. If the complaint is sufficiently comprehensive, changes in the most probable scenario with the accumulation of evidence will not require amending the complaint.

In the case of the XYZ1000 Robot, the primary causes of action would be supply of an unreasonably dangerous machine including design and manufacturing defects, failure to provide a means of preventing the Robot from harming the operator, and failure to warn that the Robot was capable of dangerous malfunction.

The allegation that the Robot had a defective widget which caused the accident might be specifically included in the original complaint, or inferred under the umbrella of design or manufacturing defects. Omitting it as a specific cause of action in the original complaint allows more scope and time for expert development of the most probable scenario during subsequent investigation. The decision to include or exclude is based on attorney preference.

Sooner or later the expert will have to commit to a final opinion as to the nature of the defects, and viable alternatives that would correct them or render them harmless. Later is better. The most probable scenario develops (and often changes) as information is gathered in the discovery process. The longer the expert can defer documenting the final opinion, the more certain that the opinion will be accurate and defensible.

Once the complaint is filed, the technical investigation of the case moves into high gear. The plaintiff's experts take the lead; the defense experts move more slowly until they know what allegations they must disprove. In-depth case research begins.

CHAPTER 5

Case Research

"Basic research is what I'm doing when I don't know what I'm doing"

—Wernher von Braun,
Attrib.

TRIED AND TRUE THEORY—THE FRYE RULE

Flawed when applied to all scientific endeavor, this quote is right on target for the purposes of forensic technology. Basic research belongs in the laboratory, not the courtroom.

The courts frown on technical theory which is neither tested by time, nor generally accepted by the scientific community. The Frye [14] decision controls expert testimony in most jurisdictions. Originally addressing the admissibility of polygraph evidence, the U.S. Court of Appeals for the D. C. Circuit ruled:

Just when a scientific principle or discovery crosses the line between experimental and demonstrable is difficult to define. . . . while courts will go a long way in admitting expert testimony deduced from a well-recognized scientific principle or discovery, the thing from which the deduction is made must . . . have gained general acceptance in the particular field in which it belongs.

The Frye rule tells experts, both plaintiff and defense, to avoid new, unique, or bizarre theories in developing most probable scenarios. Anything beyond mainstream technology will surely be attacked, disallowed, or the subject of appeal. This is particularly important when you are the only expert testifying on the basis of a specific theory, no matter how fundamental.

I once testified that a cotter pin would have improved the integrity of a bolted joint that failed, causing injury. The jury agreed. The case was appealed on the basis of the Frye decision. It was asserted that this theory had no scientific foundation, and was unsupported by other expert opinion.

The appeals court found the testimony proper, and upheld the jury decision. If the theory of failure had wandered very far from everyday technology, the decision might have been different. The Frye rule will present no problem if you stay with established theory, if you keep things technologically simple, and if you develop a scenario that does not require a convoluted explanation.

Case research for the plaintiff's expert is intended to highlight actions needed to convert prediscovery possibilities into a single most probable scenario, to support that scenario with scientific evidence, and to refute contrary scenarios.

Case research for the defense expert tries to develop a most probable scenario in which the fault is not that of the defendant, and aims at discrediting the plaintiff's scenario. The proper approach is the same for experts on both sides.

Don't use memory or experience as a substitute for the basic exploration process. Success in forensic debate demands the most accurate and up-to-date information available in the required area of expertise. As with most applied research, the best place to start is the library.

LITERATURE SEARCH

Major city and university libraries are a prolific source of technical and legal information. Many public library systems have access to the holdings of other public libraries through federally funded programs. Many of these institutions provide access to their catalog files remotely by computer modem. Florida's State University System, for example, is on-line with the Library User Information Service (LUIS).

LUIS maintains catalogs for nine university and five extension libraries. It can be queried for holdings at all of the libraries simultaneously by title or author, showing what works are available and which libraries hold them. Any library can be queried by title, author, or subject matter.

The National Technical Information Service (NTIS) in Springfield, VA catalogs and has available for sale all major unclassified technical documents prepared for or by U.S. Government agencies.

The Engineering Societies Library in New York City catalogs and maintains documents for a number of engineering associations. These include the major electrical (IEEE), mechanical (ASME), chemical (AIChE), and civil (ASCE) engineering societies. Most other technical societies such as SAE International (formerly the Society of Automotive Engineers) in Warrendale, PA, and ASTM (the American Society for Testing and Materials) in Philadelphia, PA, maintain full service libraries.

These libraries are supported by user fees, and are available to nonmembers. All offer facsimile service, and many offer on-line catalog access. Several hours spent in voice or modem communication with these sources will yield all of the latest information in any technical specialty needed to evaluate the validity of a hypothesis.

State of the art is one probative factor in determining the adequacy of products or services. Good commercial practice, as evidenced by major competitors, is usually effective as a standard. Conversely, the courts have found on occasion that entire industries failed to provide reasonably safe products by ignoring economically sound state-of-the-art technology.

The *Thomas Register of American Manufacturers*[37] is the definitive text for locating providers of both manufactured goods and commercial services. The twenty five volume, thirty thousand page directory is published annually, and is available in most public libraries. It lists all significant manufacturers in the United States, their size, their products, their locations, and their telephone numbers.

This information, together with advertisements appearing in both the directory and in the catalog volumes, identifies major competitors for almost any industrial, commercial, or consumer product or support service.

Once located, these organizations can provide sales and technical literature, both of which are useful for comparison purposes. Two caveats. First these companies will usually be more cooperative if they are unaware that their information is being used in a civil dispute, either for or against a competitor. Second, the state of the art at the time of manufacture or sale of the item rather than at some later date is the determinant.

STANDARDS, SPECIFICATIONS, AND CODES

These documents, intended to control safety and quality in products and practices, differ in their legal impact on any specific incident. The effect varies both with their source and with the rules of the court having jurisdiction.

Safety codes are generally sponsored by technical societies, and given the effect of law by inclusion in building codes or other government regulatory documents. Specifications and standards are typically created by industry and user groups, with industry representatives having the most input. Their influence on the courts appears to be somewhat less than that of codes.

Federal standards and specifications are an exception to the rule. Even when initially adopted from industry standards or specifications, their evolution comes from the most credible consumer, the United States Government. A primary function of government commodity engineers is the use of field failure data to tighten and improve both standards and specifications from the viewpoint of the consumer. This type of document development may be persuasive evidence in court with regard to product quality.

The use of codes, standards, and specifications as evidence is biased in favor of the plaintiff. The common perception is that these documents, (often through their wording), define minimum safety levels, and that noncompliance is strong evidence of an unsafe product. This is based on the concept that the courts cannot reasonably set a standard of safety below that which is established by qualified standards organizations, be they industry or government.

The natural corollary that compliance proves safety is not an effective defense in most jurisdictions because minimum safety implies a marginal product. It might be fairer to view standards as defining acceptable rather than minimum safety requirements, but this is not the real-world case.

The best defense against the allegation of noncompliance is the assertion that the product does comply either in fact, or for all practical purposes. The dispute between experts then concerns the interpretation and the intent of the document, and here the plaintiff's expert has no particular advantage. Codes, standards, and specifications can play an important part in dispute resolution. They cannot be overlooked safely by experts associated with either side.

The literature search should seek to identify all codes, standards, and specifications which may be applicable in any way to the incident under dispute. The selection often calls for some imagination.

Product advertising literature, for example, can provide clues. An indication that a commercial item was either sold to, or is on a Qualified Products List (QPL) for the United States Government implies that the product meets federal specifications and standards. Depending on the degree of truth in advertising, these documents may prove to be a help or a hindrance. In any case, they should be explored.

Most major public and university libraries maintain some sets of standards on microfilm, microfiche, or CD ROM. Information Handling Services of Englewood, CO, supplies many of these sets, but is not a source of individual documents. IHS indexes, published every few months in hard copy, are available in subscribing libraries, and provide a good starting place for identifying applicable standards and specifications for almost any product. The IHS data base includes over one hundred thousand standards from almost four hundred developing organizations.

The IHS Industry Standards and Engineering Data Subject Index for July 1991 lists standards and engineering data by subject for industry and technical associations ranging from the Aluminum Association (AA) to the Underwriters Laboratories, Inc. The single most important inclusion is ANSI, the American National Standards Institute.

ANSI develops its own standards and incorporates industrial standards promulgated by other organizations into a single large standard data base. The evolution of Standards from many small unlisted industry groups with limited standard output can often be determined after adoption into the ANSI collection.

For example, the Business and Institutional Furniture Manufacturer's Association (BIFMA) started development of a standard for office chairs in 1974. The starting point was a 1955 Federal Specification (AA-C-293) for office chairs. This group developed and tested a chair standard between 1974 and 1984.

The standard was submitted to ANSI in 1984, resulting in the issuance of ANSI standard ANSI/BIFMA X5.1-1985, General Purpose Office Chairs—Tests. The expert, concerned with the adequacy of a chair built prior to 1985, can use the IHS index to identify and acquire the 1985 ANSI standard. This leads backward to unlisted standards that existed previously. These can then be gotten from appropriate sources.

The IHS Locator Index for the U.S. Government Specifications Service is a primary identifier for federal standards, handbooks, specifications, drawings, and qualified products lists. Most large libraries are now depositories for government documents, and can provide or procure copies of specific documents. In the absence of this service, a call to the National Technical Information Service will either provide the document or identify an appropriate source.

SPECIAL SOURCES

There are several litigation specific sources of data which are important in any forensic investigation. These deal directly with the frequency of occurrence, circumstances, and outcome of incidents similar to that under investigation.

First is the informal briefing or more formal seminar limited to house counsel and defense counsel for major industrial entities. Here defense counsel is made aware of previous disputes, theories, winning and losing strategies, experts both pro and con together with their effectiveness, and full documentation for each case. This information is available to the defense experts. Plaintiff's counsel is privy only to that trivial portion of the information revealed in the answers to interrogatories.

Plaintiff's counsel has a comparable weapon. The Association of Trial Lawyers of America (ATLA) declares a part of its mission is "to champion the cause of those who deserve redress for injury to person or property." This eliminates most defense attorneys. ATLA maintains a massive data base containing identifying information about cases and judgements in all areas of trial law. This information is available to plaintiff's counsel.

Once a similar case is identified, a second part of the ATLA mission takes effect, "to encourage cooperation among members." Most member attorneys will support their counterparts with full documentation, equivalent to what is supplied by defendant industries to defense counsel.

This may consist of multiple file boxes of documents including complaints, interrogatories, depositions, trial transcripts, photographs, videotapes, and any other material not restrained by court order or settlement agreement. This becomes available to the plaintiff's expert, and may cast light on the incident under investigation beyond what the expert has already developed.

The two major on-line commercial data bases devoted to the law are Lexis by Meade Data Central, and Westlaw by West Publishing Co. They are both excellent sources of case history and legal precedent. Unfortunately the high cost of these services makes them uneconomical except for large firms with expert computer users. With user fees in excess of two hundred dollars per hour, data base browsing becomes an expensive exercise for the uninitiated. If the service is available through the client attorney, it can provide valuable information.

There are a number of special purpose federal government data bases which can be accessed free of charge, or for a nominal fee. These include, among others, accident tabulations by the Consumer Product Safety Commission, the U.S. Department of Transportation, and OSHA, all in the Washington, DC area. They are usually less rewarding than the sources previously described, but they do occasionally turn up a gem.

Data collection can continue endlessly, depending on the complexity and economics of the case and on the ease of access to information. Stop when you have the information you need; keep looking if you don't. Overkill in the literature search can confuse the case, the client, and the jury. Use your best judgement to decide when to stop accumulating information and start analyzing it.

THE SOFT SCENARIO—THEORY OR HYPOTHESIS

Completion of the literature search permits the development of a probable soft scenario, a scenario based solely on documentary and visual information gathered by the expert at this time. In many cases the soft scenario is supported by enough evidence to accept it as a most probable hard (or final) scenario without further effort. However, there are often compelling reasons to proceed to a testing program for evaluation or demonstration purposes.

The "what next" decision depends largely on whether the soft scenario is, strictly defined, a theory or a hypothesis. Theory, for our purposes, is a more or less verified or established explanation accounting for known facts. Hypothesis is conjecture put forth as a possible explanation which serves as a basis of experiment by which to reach the truth.

If the soft scenario is a hypothesis, verification testing is mandatory. Newton[29] stated this proposition in a manner suited to forensic work,

"I frame no hypotheses; for whatever is not deduced from the phenomena . . . has no place in experimental philosophy." The use of a hypothesis as a theory can lead to exclusion under the Frye rule, or attack by other equally likely hypotheses or more likely theories.

It is not enough to say "this might have happened." The only credible position for the expert in court is "this is what I think did happen." Hypotheses must be tested if the expert is to render a probative opinion. If the soft scenario is a theory which is complex and difficult to convey to a lay court, testing for demonstrative purposes may be desirable. The decision to test a theory is optional, and can be made by the client attorney who will factor into the equation the tradeoff between economics and courtroom effectiveness.

Whether performed for exploratory or for demonstrative purposes, forensic testing has special protocols which must be observed to maintain the integrity of evidence samples, the admissability of test results, and the composure of the expert under cross-examination.

Most otherwise qualified test personnel are unfamiliar with these special requirements. Thus, the forensic expert maintains final responsibility for assuring that testing meets courtroom standards for either developing or supporting a most probable scenario.

CHAPTER 6

Test and Evaluation

"He therefore who wishes to rejoice without doubt in regard to the truths underlying phenomena must know how to devote himself to experiment."

—Roger Bacon,
Opus Majus

TESTS PLAY NO FAVORITES

Test results are unpredictable. Early in my experience as a test engineer I would speculate that certain tests were unnecessary, either because the test item was sure to pass or sure to fail. I was wrong often enough to cure me of this habit very quickly.

You should be ready for unfavorable results. If you are unprepared to accept an adverse test result, you probably should avoid the test. Recognize, however, that competent opposition will probably run the test and interpret the results in the most damaging way possible.

There are two valid thoughts in test planning and the evaluation of test results which appear antithetic, but aren't. The first is that a preconceived theory creates a tendency to twist the interpretation of test results to suit it. The second is that if the truth is known, proof by testing should be easy.

Because of these concepts some caution is essential when selecting and interpreting tests. Don't be prejudiced by your hopes during test selection. Don't let a preconception of the "truth" bias your thinking during evaluation. Don't predict the results. Fit the theory to data rather than the data to theory.

Slanted or selective testing is frequently used to support a tenuous position, particularly in support of advertising claims. Forensic testing, subject to vigorous and expert attack, cannot afford such bias. Thus, most testing in support of litigation is performed in accordance with good test practice. Test results and evaluation are not always treated with the same respect. The result of "cooked" test interpretation is often an adverse decision by the courts.

Participating as a consultant, I had the opportunity to observe two well-qualified metallurgists dispute in court the interpretation of their test data. The case revolved about the identification of a specific truck as the one involved in a night hit and run collision with a motorcycle. The crux of the dispute was whether streaks on the steel truck wheel were aluminum, and whether they came from the broken motorcycle fork, or from aluminum paint.

Both experts had independently analyzed the extraneous wheel material using electron microscopy. The test results were similar; the material was aluminum with a fairly high silicon content. The analysis was consistent with the high silicon aluminum casting alloy used in motorcycle forks. The defense expert seemed to have formed a preconception that the aluminum paint theory was valid, despite the fact that aluminum paint usually contains little or no silicon.

Probably trying to fit the facts to the theory, the following statements had been made at various times by this expert while being deposed.

> What I was seeing was predominantly aluminum paint . . . It contains a lot more silicon than any aluminum paint that I've ever seen, but that could be an answer, I suppose they could have used aluminum alloy to make that paint pigment to have more silicon in it . . . That's my guess, they used cheap scrap aluminum and made the paint from that source.

The defense paint theory now required that the paint be made from high silicon aluminum scrap such as would be found in broken motorcycle forks. This testimony, fitting the test results to a theory, was highlighted during cross-examination at trial. It was undoubtedly one of the reasons the jury found for the plaintiff.

TEST PLANNING—LABORATORY SELECTION

Testing can be complex and expensive. Development of a well conceived test plan assures cost effective testing, produces data that can withstand assault, and minimizes the possible need for damage control when tests generate "wrong" answers.

The laboratory is a natural working environment for most experts in the sciences. Testing applied to their specialties is usually within the scope of their expertise. Testing outside of their specialties is better implemented by conferring with test experts operating the laboratory facilities necessary for their tests.

Their engineering counterparts are usually oriented more toward the practical aspects of design, development, and production. Engineers normally rely on test specialists for assistance in test planning, testing, and test evaluation of their work product.

Both the scientist and the engineer can benefit from test expert consultation in designing and implementing a forensic test program. The single most important factor for assuring good test design is interaction with experienced test personnel in a qualified laboratory. It is part of the job of the expert to identify them. Assuming the expert has no suitable in-house laboratory, many contract facilities with trained test personnel are available. Most of them do good work. Some don't.

The final responsibility for qualifying the laboratory, selecting tests, test supervision, and result evaluation remains with the expert. If a test sample from an accident is given to a laboratory for unsupervised testing, there are two undesirable results. First, the chain of custody of evidence has been weakened. Second, the person performing the test is now needed as a witness to the handling of evidence, the methods of testing, and the significance of results. Keeping these factors in mind, begin test plan development.

Start by noting the things that you want to find out, and the things that you want to demonstrate. The preliminary plan may call for field testing, for laboratory testing, or both. The logical sequence of events is preliminary test planning, laboratory selection, final test planning, test implementation, and test result evaluation.

ASTM Standard E-860-82 provides guidelines for examining and testing items involved in products liability litigation. The rules are not specific to any particular type of testing, but there are enough administrative warnings included to make the document worthwhile reading before making test plans.

Laboratory selection is based on the type of information needed, which translates to the type of testing to be performed. It is possible to identify candidate laboratories without knowing specifically what tests you want, and what equipment is needed to perform them. Starting cold, the best source book is the *ASTM Directory of Testing Laboratories.*[1]

This annual publication lists over a thousand laboratories by location in the United States, with several hundred others world wide. It describes their specialties, fields of testing, equipment, personnel, and contact information. The capabilities are sorted into sixteen fields of testing, including chemical, electrical, mechanical, metrology, nondestructive, microscopy, and others.

The labs are further classified into seven types of service, one of which is forensic. The forensic laboratories can usually offer failure analysis and expert testimony, if required. They are aware of the problems of the expert witness, and can be expected to provide technical assistance in the selection of tests and presentation of results. All other things being equal, the choice of a laboratory with forensic experience is desirable.

Finally, the entries are identified by twelve major categories and fifty-eight subcategories of materials and products. These listings cover all reasonable needs of a technical expert witness for test services. They do not vouch for the quality and adequacy of the personnel and the facility. That determination remains to be done by the expert needing the service.

Contact apparently suitable candidate laboratories and get technical and price information, preferably in the form of technical sales literature. This usually narrows the field. Then visit the facilities and talk to the people. Some ideas about things to look for, and questions to ask are found in ASTM Standard E994-84, "Guide for Laboratory Accreditation Systems."

Ask what tests they would propose, the significance of the results, the equipment to be used, the available alternatives, and the estimated time and cost. Be certain that you will be able to witness and approve of each step of the testing.

Your selection task is easier if the laboratory performs work for the United States Government either directly or as a subcontractor. This indicates that the laboratory has passed a facility survey with regard to personnel and equipment, that its control of test quality is adequate, and that its periodic instrument calibration is traceable to the National Bureau of Standards.

Alternately, the laboratory may be accredited by some other responsible source. The American Association for Laboratory Accreditation of

Gaithersburg, Maryland is a nonprofit organization devoted to assuring that member laboratories meet the criteria specified in the international standard, ISO/IEC Guide 25-82. This standard, "General Requirements for the Technical Competence of Testing Laboratories," offers assurance of laboratory quality adequate for the demands of the courts.

Once the laboratory is chosen, the test plan should be revised to its final form with laboratory assistance. It should identify the tests to be run, the test sequence, the data to be collected, the instrumentation to be used, and documentation procedures. It should also include logic analysis, indicating which tests might produce results which would alter the test program.

A program might be terminated either because a theory had been sufficiently proved, or because a hypothesis had been found improbable. Or the results may be ambiguous, calling for retests or new tests to establish the truth. In any case, the test plan should consider what alternate actions might be taken at any point in the program depending on early results.

Truly unbiased, you should develop as complete a test plan as is economically consistent with the investigation. The tests should be designed to support your position if it is correct. You are under no obligation to specify tests designed to weaken your theories. The cost and effort to do that is the obligation of your adversaries.

FIELD TESTING

Site inspection and field testing usually overlap in scope and location, and frequently are carried out simultaneously. They are, however, two distinct operations. Site inspection is an integral part of most investigations by both plaintiff and defense experts. Field testing, as the term is used here, means testing and operation of the allegedly defective device in order to try to duplicate the failure suspected of causing the injury.

Some testing may be required during site inspection. These tests typically involve laboratory type measurements such as light levels, noise levels, coefficients of friction, etc. The techniques required for good laboratory testing are well documented, and equally applicable here. The techniques for field testing of an allegedly defective machine or device are indefinite, vary with the circumstances surrounding the accident, and rely heavily on the experience and ingenuity of the expert.

Ideally, field testing requires that the allegedly defective device be operational and not substantially altered since the incident in dispute. It further requires full access by test personnel for periods long enough to instrument the device, make adjustments, operate in various modes, and document the results by photographic or other means.

If the devices are used for industrial purposes, strict time restrictions may be put on access. Under these conditions testing has to be "quick and dirty," or testing must be performed on an exemplar machine obtained through other channels. You may not be able to field test to your complete satisfaction. Do the best you can with whatever resources are available.

I had occasion to work on a case involving a propane explosion in a hotel pool heating system. The explosion was allegedly caused by a pressure regulator valve leaking propane to the atmosphere prior to the ignition of a pilot light. The valve had been disassembled by an adverse expert prior to my involvement.

A nick was present in the edge of the valve disk, and this was alleged to be the cause of the suspected propane leak. The valve was supplied to me as a box of parts together with the adverse report. Visually, the nick didn't look bad enough to cause the amount of leakage necessary to develop an explosive mixture in the pool house.

The valve was reassembled using the defective disk, and reinstalled in the pool system with the cooperation of the owners. The system showed no detectable leakage when tested with a sensitive hydrocarbon detector at normal operating pressure, and no leakage when tested at five times normal operating pressure. The system then ran through several operating cycles, performing flawlessly.

The more logical theory was developed that a piping leak downstream of the pressure regulator dropped the outlet line pressure, causing the regulator to deliver propane in accordance with its normal function. This theory was tested and proved valid by cracking a fitting beyond the valve to permit leakage. The valve then acted as predicted. The court was influenced more by this theory supported by an operational field test than by the hypothesis supported by laboratory examination. The finding was for the defendant.

In another case an idling forklift with a hydraulic transmission went from neutral to forward without an operator on board. A fork severely injured a worker unloading the lift. The defense alleged that the forklift had been left in gear, and that unloading caused it to move. The forklift had been scrapped and used for parts when I was introduced to the case.

Field testing was done on a similar model lift at the accident site. There was a position in the shifter, as designed, where the transmission gave every evidence that it was in neutral, but was not positively locked in position. Engine vibration allowed the transmission to shift into forward after a period of time long enough to let the operator leave the lift and start unloading.

Although certain available parts of the old lift were subjected to laboratory examination to help support the theory, videotapes of the auto-operation of the similar lift in the field played an important part in influencing the jury. The finding was for the plaintiff.

Field testing of the imaginary XYZ1000 Robot would undoubtedly present problems because we assumed it to be back in the production process. A proper test would involve taking the machine out of production, installing a defective widget, and determining how the robot would function. Precautions would have to be taken to assure the accident itself did not reoccur.

The probability of being permitted a field test of this magnitude on production machinery is low. Working for the defense, an exemplar machine would probably be made available by the manufacturer for testing. Working for the plaintiff, it might be possible to gain access to an exemplar machine by rental. It is more probable that the resolution of this case would revolve about laboratory testing of the broken widget.

The effectiveness of field testing lies in its ability to communicate bottom-line technical information to a lay jury without the need for explanation. It is frequently necessary to supplement or replace this type of testing with laboratory testing. Here the requirements are more structured, the emphasis is on test technology, and the significance of the results may require extensive explanation in court.

LABORATORY TESTING

Many test organizations can perform what we have described as field or operational testing, either in the field or in the laboratory. The term "laboratory testing," as used here, indicates tests that explore the physical characteristics of evidence for purposes of identification, or tests of parts to establish failure modes.

The final test plan will have selected a few appropriate tests from a very large menu of possibilities. Even a simple test, such as determining the hardness of a steel sample, can be performed using various modifications of Brinell, Vickers, Rockwell, Scleroscope, and Pendulum equipment. The selection must be made on the basis of judgment and experience. The results will be comparable only when the instruments selected measure the same macro characteristics.

When the measurements require more advanced test equipment, the possible permutations and areas for disagreement are greater. Consider the problem of determining the composition and nature of a metallic fragment which cannot be destroyed because of its evidentiary nature.

Possible nondestructive test methods include scanning or transmission electron microscopy, X-ray diffraction analysis, energy dispersive or wavelength dispersive X-ray spectroscopy, auger microprobe analysis, and others. The choice of methods by the testifying expert should certainly be made with guidance from laboratory personnel except under extraordinary conditions.

The principal role of the testifying expert is that of test supervisor. The test procedure must be fully understood, the tests properly documented, and the results unambiguous. Most important, the results must be formulated in a manner designed to convince a jury of their truth and significance. Failure to do that resulted in the loss of a suit in which I am certain to this day that my client, the defendant, had no liability.

The case involved a twin-engine aircraft which had undergone overhaul of both engines at a commercial maintenance facility. Several days later, during takeoff, a failure of one engine resulted in a fatal crash with resulting fire. Government investigators determined the cause to be a carburetor gasket which they alleged had gone through a solvent cleaning bath with the carburetor, and had not been replaced. They based this finding on the hardened (but not distorted) condition of the gasket after the crash and fire.

Laboratory tests on new gaskets clearly proved two things. First, a new gasket placed in the solvent became so badly softened and distorted that it would have been impossible to reinstall with the carburetor. Second, a new gasket placed in a 300 degree fahrenheit oven for a few minutes hardened, and appeared identical to the gasket retrieved from the fire.

It was obvious to me that the after-crash fire caused the gasket to harden, rather than the hardened gasket causing the aircraft to crash.

I explained this to a jury, certain that the truth would prevail. They apparently didn't believe me, and found for the plaintiff. I should have presented the evidence differently.

Those tests could have been run on the witness stand with a jar of solvent, a hair drier, and two new gaskets. I believe, in retrospect, that the impact of the same tests carried out in front of the jury would have resulted in a different verdict.

It was a hard lesson, but one never forgotten. The purpose of testing is initially to inform an expert, but ultimately to convince a jury. If it fails to do both, it is an exercise in futility. Hold that thought, both while planning tests and while testing.

EVALUATING TEST RESULTS

Test results that are confusing, misleading, or irrelevant, may be inadmissible as evidence. A properly planned and executed test program will produce results that are clear and germane, and that can provide a solid basis for expert opinion.

ASTM Standard E678-84, "Standard Practice for Evaluation of Technical Data," establishes some principles for the analysis of test results. Its defined scope is "the evaluation of technical data, appropriate criteria for such evaluation, and other relevant considerations which constitute a proper basis for the formation of technical opinions in product liability matters."

The document advocates unbiased testing, careful documentation of data, statistical analysis of results, and the application of sound technical practice in evaluation. Dealing primarily in broad generalities, it does provide some good thoughts about appropriate methodology for test planning as well as result evaluation.

The essence of good forensic evaluation practice can be summed up in a few simple rules. Be sure that the test results are directed toward a specific element of the complaint. Be sure that the data are precise and reproducible. Be sure that the data are adequate to permit drawing the necessary conclusions. Be sure that the data are consistent with other factual evidence. Finally, be sure that the significance of the data can be easily understood by nontechnical people.

CHAPTER 7

The Most Probable Scenario

"In an argument, the difficulty lies not in being able to defend your position, but in knowing it."

—Andre Maurois,
Magiciens et Logiciens

A TIME FOR DELIBERATION

Test and evaluation complete, you probably know as much as you ever will about the technical aspects of the case. It's time now to develop a fixed position that you are willing and able to defend against certain onslaught.

"When you have eliminated the impossible, whatever remains, however improbable, must be the truth." So said Sherlock Holmes.[8] What remains in real life are a number of "truths," all having some degree of probability, and many being mutually exclusive. The problem at this point is to combine those truths which are germane, mutually compatible, and clearly logical, into a theory defining your "most probable scenario."

There is occasional pressure to adopt a theory conceived by the client attorney as a "most probable scenario." Don't let this pressure cloud your judgment. Unquestioned acceptance of a designated theory is a risky bet. You may win some, but you will certainly lose others that you shouldn't.

If the client theory is correct, you will be able to arrive at it independently. If not, your own theory may be more favorable or less favorable to the case, but it will certainly be more easily defended. At this point review all the evidence to refresh your memory, organize the material so it is easily understood, and start to prepare a position as conclusive as possible. Take your time, and think long and carefully. Winning or losing depends heavily on the final opinions and theories you are about to construct.

ANALYSIS OF THE EVIDENCE

It was noted previously that the sheer volume of evidence to be reviewed before fixing a technical opinion in a high-value case can be awesome. Hundreds of pages of complaints and amendments, interrogatories and answers, technical documentation, and early investigative reports are only the beginning.

Lay witnesses will have been deposed offering new and often contradictory evidence. In a case involving a fatal industrial accident, I read the depositions of fourteen lay witnesses consisting of more than fifteen hundred pages of transcribed testimony before examining the accident site. If opposing experts have been deposed before you are required to disclose your final opinion, you may have to consider hundreds of additional pages of technical testimony.

Your case file is probably going to be inspected by opposition attorneys at your deposition. The file should be free of extraneous and misleading material. Once again, you have an obligation to answer all questions truthfully. You have no obligation to tell your opponents what questions to ask. If you have followed the advice of chapter four, "keep a log, not a diary," your file will be clean up to this point. Try to keep it that way.

Although it is not uncommon to "sanitize" a file before deposition by removal or alteration of material, such action is improper. While it is probably acceptable to transcribe your interim notes into a more legible and clearer form while discarding the originals, it is more effective just to refrain from writing anything you would not wish used against you.

You will be familiar with most of the mass of material you are about to review. The following approach, or some modification of it, should prove useful in extracting and summarizing all the important information without excessive written documentation.

First, skim through all the depositions to recall the people, their relationships to the incident, and the importance of their testimony. Most of the depositions will describe the accident, or the scene after the accident. They will not affect your analysis, except as they elaborate on the accident reports. It is sufficient to list without comment the names and the relationships of these deponents for future reference. Then set these marginal documents aside.

Next, carefully review those depositions you feel provide data important to your analysis, both favorable and unfavorable to your client. Some important testimony will have been identified during your earlier study. More will now become apparent as a result of new evidence developed since your first reading. Mark the important pages and lines with paper clips, or identify the pages with adhesive note markers. Again, do not make notes or marks directly on the documents, because they would then take on new significance and become the heaviest part of the case file required at your deposition.

Finally, review all the other legal and technical documentation to refresh your memory and to absorb any new information that appears relevant. Mark this documentation with paper clips or "post-its," and set aside any documents not necessary for substantiating your final opinion.

CONSIDER ALL THE POSSIBILITIES

The "most probable scenario" in a civil case is rarely obvious beyond a reasonable doubt. There will be a number of possible scenarios, some more probable than others. You should consider all reasonable possibilities before theorizing.

Returning to the XYZ1000 Robot, we attributed the accident to a defective widget. Before reaching this conclusion, it would have been necessary to eliminate (among other things) the possibilities of operator error, alterations or removal of safety devices, abuse of the machine, failure of hydraulic, pneumatic, mechanical or electrical systems, microprocessor malfunction, or stray input signals.

It would not be sufficient to offer the widget as a possible cause of the accident. It would also be necessary to provide evidence both that the widget was the principal culprit (proximate cause), and that the other factors were not major contributors to the accident.

A sound "most probable scenario" must include and account for all of the evidence; or alternately, that portion of the evidence which does not support the scenario must be discredited. The adverse evidence may be accurate, or it may be a result of erroneous observation by lay witnesses, misconception by expert witnesses, or perjury.

The less exception taken to the evidence as it exists, the better. However, most civil cases that reach trial will offer a choice of scenarios based on conflicting evidence. It is the function of the expert to note the aberrant evidence as early as possible, and to explain the anomaly to the client attorney. It is the function of the attorney to discredit the adverse evidence if possible, both during the deposition of opponents and at trial.

Reviewing the evidence you have marked, start to formulate two possible scenarios, one the most favorable to your client (the best possible scenario), and the other the least favorable (the worst possible scenario). Make brief notes about all evidence supporting your best possible scenario. Remember, without notation, any contrary evidence.

START FROM THE TOP

Evaluate the best possible scenario in terms of the evidence in order to create a "best" theory of the accident. Where there is adverse evidence you are unable to refute, make such changes to your theory as are necessary to accommodate that evidence. Conceding as little as possible, alter the best possible scenario to create a theory of the "best" most probable scenario.

Spend some time with your "best" theory. Review it until you are certain that you understand it thoroughly, that you can state it succinctly, and that you have instant recall of the evidence for it and the evidence against it.

Look for obvious flaws in the theory. You will shortly have a chance to analyze your position in depth, and to change your mind. For now have a theory with which you are comfortable. If you are unable to do this now, you are probably better off stopping work at this point and resigning from the case. Assuming you have developed an acceptable theory, it's time to switch positions.

PLAY THE DEVIL'S ADVOCATE

Having constructed two opposing scenarios, you should evaluate them impartially. Because you hope, consciously or subconsciously, that the best possible scenario will prevail, it's hard to be unbiased. Force yourself to treat the least favorable scenario fairly, either by playing the devil's advocate yourself, or by using a knowledgeable associate to play that role.

In most cases you will play your own opposition for two reasons. First, associates with the necessary skills are rare, and the time needed to tell them all you know about a case can be excessive. Second, you may be asked at deposition to identify anyone with whom you discussed the case, and thus face the possibility of them being deposed as potential witnesses.

Now evaluate the worst possible scenario in terms of the evidence. Imagine that you have been retained by the opposition, and that the worst possible scenario is now your ideal position. Make the strongest case that you can considering all of the evidence. Repeat the process used to establish a "best" theory of the accident to mentally create a "worst" theory of the accident. Again modify the worst possible scenario to accommodate irrefutable evidence adverse to it, thus developing a theory of a "worst" most probable scenario.

Examine it for possible flaws. Study and remember it. Don't devote the effort to planning the worst case that you have to the best case, and don't write down your analysis. If the worst case ultimately prevails in your thinking, you will probably not be called as an expert witness, and any further association with either side of the case will be most unlikely.

CONVINCE YOURSELF OR EXCUSE YOURSELF

You now have a "best" and a "worst" most probable scenario. Compare them point by point. Imagine yourself in the position of a member of a debating team assigned to defend first one position, and then the other. Summarize for yourself the salient points you would attempt to make for each of the positions. Talk aloud in front of a mirror or into a tape recorder, if it helps.

Consider what questions you would ask as an attorney seeking to discredit each of the positions. Decide if there are credible answers to those questions, and how you would answer them. Repeat this process as often as necessary until you have a clear understanding of both sides of the case.

Now imagine yourself as a juror, and assume you don't understand those technical aspects of the case which are the basis of the expert testimony. Further assume that two equally credible experts are going to present you with the two conflicting most probable scenarios. As objectively as possible, determine which of the arguments would be more credible to you.

The answer to that question establishes your preferential position. If the worst scenario dominates, it's time to talk to your client about resigning from the case. If the best scenario dominates, it means that you are convinced your client position is probably correct, and it's time for in-depth analysis.

REINFORCE AND REPORT YOUR POSITION

The levels of proof have been described as "beyond a reasonable doubt" (90%+ probability), "clear and convincing evidence" (75%+ probability), and "more likely than not" (50%+ probability). If your confidence of proof in the "best" most probable scenario at this point is less than "clear and convincing," further deliberation is in order.

The danger of fitting facts to theories rather than theories to facts has been noted. As Leroux[24] wrote, "it is dangerous, very dangerous . . . to go from a preconceived idea to find the proofs to fit it." Paradoxically, once you determine that your theory is correct, ambivalent facts frequently fall into place. Quoting Paul,[31] "once the truth is known, it becomes easier to prove it."

Walking a careful line between these two maxims, you should be able to bolster your position until you are satisfied that your theory is based on clear and convincing proof. Appearing in an adversarial setting with less than this level of certainty leaves you vulnerable to attack by opposing counsel.

Having reached a firm and favorable position, review your findings with your client attorney orally. Describe in detail both the positive and negative factors that went into your thinking. Omit nothing. The more familiar attorneys are with both the pros and cons of a technical argument, the better they are able to determine which issues they wish to try.

Until now your notes have been cryptic and minimal, and you have prepared no formal report. Some jurisdictions require a report by a testifying expert. Where the report is not mandatory, the client can now decide whether or not a formal report is desirable. As a general rule, the client will request a report where serious settlement negotiations are anticipated, and decline a report where litigation is the probable outcome.

Your report should be succinct and should contain no material indicating areas of vulnerability. It should describe what evidence you have reviewed, and your conclusions based on that evidence. Occasionally it may be necessary to include a brief statement on theory to make the report intelligible.

In summary, say what you have to say as concisely as possible, offer no openings for attack, and offer no gratuitous information. A suitable report format is shown in Appendix C. The format is typical, and may be altered to fit the style or needs of the individual.

You are now about ready to become an active participant in the battle. You've spent a lot of time and done a number of things getting to this point. During this period the opposition hasn't been idly standing by. It's time to consider what they probably have been doing to prepare for you.

CHAPTER 8

Before the Deposition

"How goes the enemy?"

—Frederic Reynolds,
The Dramatist

THE ENEMY GAME PLAN

Other than by chance, there are some people whom you haven't met up to now who don't have your best interests at heart. Moreover, they probably know a lot about you, although not as much as they will know after your deposition. These people are the opposing counsel and the opposing experts.

Opposing counsel has been busily countering the legal maneuvers of your own client attorney. Most of these activities affect you only marginally, but you are not forgotten. One of the highest priorities of opposing attorneys is to destroy your credibility in court. First they have to find out who you are, and what you are going to say. They do this to some extent by filing "expert interrogatories."

The interrogatories will ask for your name and address, your field of alleged expertise, your education and work background, your publications, and your years of experience. They will ask what your opinions are, what resources you used in reaching them, whether you have test results, whether you submitted any written reports, and a host of other questions.

Your client attorney will delay releasing this information as long as possible with such statements as "we have a number of potential trial witnesses, but until we know who the opposition witnesses are and the nature of their testimony, we can't identify which experts we will call to testify at trial." But ultimately you will be identified to your adversaries some time before your deposition. Now opposition inquiry starts.

Don't underestimate your antagonists. They are probably as knowledgeable as you, as skillful as you, and may well be more crafty and less scrupulous. Moreover, the higher the stakes, the more adept and well studied the opponents will usually be. At least that's the safest assumption to make. When it's wrong, as sometimes happens, the results are usually gratifying. Nevertheless, be prepared for an unfriendly examination of your credentials and opinions.

Your background will be searched for weaknesses. Expect your school records to be examined, your work history to be investigated, and your credit standing to be checked. None of these things may happen, but they sometimes do. Any weaknesses found will be saved as a surprise for the courtroom. Practicing as an expert witness is probably one of the few areas of endeavor in which a little paranoia is healthy.

Once, at the height of the cold war, I had occasion to do some firestorm testing of residential basement fallout shelters for the New York State Civil Defense Commission. Because the incendiary material in residential firestorm would be house wreckage, the test was performed using that material for fuel. Shelter personnel safety was determined by monitoring for internal temperatures, oxygen levels, and the presence of noxious gases. It was, in fact, a well conceived and implemented test.

Almost twenty years later, while testifying in a case of alleged arson, opposing counsel attempted to discredit that experience by asking "isn't it true that you just threw some old junk wood on the shelters and set it on fire?" Apparently some good investigative work turned up the old report, and the question caught me off guard. It took some quick memory search and careful phrasing to convince the jury that the experiment was technically sound.

Don't be intimidated by this opposition research. You can be an effective expert in areas where you have special knowledge even though that specialty forms a small part of your overall skills. There is no problem in selecting and presenting those areas of your education and experience which document your expertise in a specific and limited area. Just be sure that the background factors you select are accurate, relevant, and will withstand full investigation.

TECHNICAL INQUIRY

A good opposing counsel will use his investigators and his experts to analyze what technical positions you have previously taken. If your experience has been limited to non-forensic activities, this analysis will depend on what you have written for professional purposes, or what you have said in recorded technical lectures. As you gain forensic experience, the nature of the investigation becomes more intense.

Except for confidentiality through agreement by the settling parties, or through a protective order by the courts, most things that you have said under oath are part of the public record. Assume that they will be examined by your opponents for inconsistencies. Assume especially that they will be examined for contradiction with your present opinions as described in the expert interrogatories.

Expert practice is primarily of two types, specialized and generalized. Where there have been many incidents of the same type, for example, Ford Pinto rear-end collision fires, an expert can testify many times in many forums to the same scenario expressing the same opinions. Where the coverage is broader, for example machinery failures of all types, the scenarios and opinions may vary substantially from case to case.

With time, you can qualify as an expert in many diverse areas having a common, but not obvious, technical heritage. A good attorney will try to take advantage of this at trial to cast doubt on your expertise by portraying you as a "jack of all trades, master of none." Sincerity, honesty, solid technical knowledge, and planned communication techniques usually render this ploy ineffective. Nevertheless, count on your past testimony being available to opposing counsel. Also count on it being carefully reviewed for weakness by persons expert in your field.

After several courtroom appearances, you will probably have displayed some strengths and some weaknesses in demeanor and courtroom relationships. You will have left an impression on both friendly and adverse counsel as to your overall skill and effectiveness. Your new opposition counsel will probably solicit opinions from your previous opponents regarding the degree of threat you pose, things to avoid in questioning you, and any weaknesses in your technique which might be exploited.

Again, the ultimate goal of the opposition is casting doubt on your credibility as an expert in court. And again, good witness skills and adequate preparation render this type of attack ineffective. Be sure, prior to your deposition, to study transcripts of your testimony in any cases having a technical basis in any way similar to the current case. Read them with the same jaundiced eye that an opponent would, and you will be prepared for whatever happens.

ADVERSARIAL DEPOSITION PLANNING

Opposing counsel has a logical strategy when developing a pattern of questions for your deposition. You can ultimately be attacked in court on three levels. First is your qualification as an expert. Second is the validity and accuracy of your opinions. Finally, all else failing, is your character. The adversary approach to a deposition is designed to provide material which may later be used in court for any or all of these purposes.

The opposition agenda will typically be designed to provide new information, or to expand on already known information concerning your personal life, your background, your education, your work history, and any proclivity on your part to be an activist for either plaintiffs or defendants. It will be aimed at developing data to weaken your claimed expertise.

Next it will try to establish exactly what your opinions are, and how sure you are of them. The opposition will attempt to force you into immutable technical positions which can be dissected at leisure by opposing experts. It is in the best interests of the opposition to paint you into a corner where any change in position (even based on new information) will weaken the impact of your courtroom testimony.

Attempts will be made to get concessions on your part, no matter how slight, concerning the probability of alternative scenarios more favorable to the opposition than your own. Further attempts will be made to trap you into inconsistencies by asking the same question in several different ways, hoping for contradictory answers. Finally the opposing counsel will use the deposition to make a personal evaluation of your probable effectiveness as a hostile witness.

As they evaluate you, opposing attorneys usually avoid giving you a preview of what to expect from them at trial. They will usually be cordial, soft-spoken, and appreciative of your helping their understanding of the case. Expect no histrionics in the questioning, and expect no reaction to your answers. But don't be surprised if a lawyer who is a pussy cat in a deposition becomes a full grown tiger in court.

The only reasonably sure analysis of adversary trial technique and skill will come from discussion with your own client attorney. Good attorneys know the opponent's professional performance either personally or by reputation, and they will certainly try to share this knowledge with you.

GETTING READY

The deposition will be your first exposure to enemy fire. Careful preparation will prevent giving away gratuitous information and making unnecessary concessions during the deposition. Moreover, good planning can leave the opposition with the impression of you that best suits your client's intent.

If your client attorney feels there is no good probability of settlement, the less formidable the opposition considers you before trial, the better. If, on the other hand, your client doesn't want to try the case, but intends to take the best settlement available, your cause is best served by a forceful and convincing manner while being deposed.

Prior to being deposed, review your case file until you are completely familiar with every item in it. Know why each one is in your file, and what bearing, if any, each had in forming your opinions. If you have followed the guidelines previously described, the file will be clean, germane, and nonredundant. If it is not, discuss the file with your client. If it can be sanitized ethically, do so. If not, be prepared to justify the extraneous material.

Formulate the most difficult questions you can envision to attack your own theories, and then consider carefully how you would respond to each. The truth is always the truth, but the format of a truthful response to a difficult question can lead your opponent to or away from a particular area of exploration.

Review the case thoroughly with your client attorney. Find out how your testimony fits into the overall case. Determine what parts of your testimony are critical, and what scenario the opposition will attempt to have you concede. Have your client question you in a manner similar to what you can expect from the opposing counsel during deposition, and get a critique of each of your answers.

Be sure your client understands the full import of what you intend to say. Most trial lawyers are exposed to so many different technical disciplines in their work that they sometimes are unaware of the technical significance of a single piece of evidence or opinion. They must, and most often do, rely on their technical experts to give them a crash course in applicable technology.

The time for this instruction is just before deposition, and again just before the evidence is to be introduced at trial. Never assume that what is clear to you is clear to anyone else. Make sure your client understands your position completely and that no significant part of your testimony has been overlooked.

"DO AND DON'T" DEPOSITION GUIDELINES

There is a school of thought in the legal profession which holds that the best tactics for an expert witness are the same for a deposition as they are for courtroom testimony. I disagree.

While many principles are common to both arenas, it is important to remember that a deposition results in hard copy on paper, while courtroom testimony usually results in impressions left in the minds of a jury. For this reason the guidance provided here for a prospective witness before deposition is not universally applicable to a witness preparing for trial.

Things to Do

1. Tell the truth. First you will be under oath to do so. Second you should assume that any false or inaccurate response will be detected, exposed, and used to destroy your credibility at trial.

2. Make sure you understand each question. Questions can be confusing, misleading, or compound (two or more questions in one). Unless the question is absolutely clear to you, ask for clarification before answering.

3. Respond only to what you are asked. If you anticipate where opposing counsel is going with a line of questioning and try to preempt that line with your answers, you may be doing the opposition's work for them. Answer the question and stop. If the opposition wants more information, make them ask for it.

4. Take your time before answering, no matter how long it takes. Your answer will be transcribed, and the transcription does not indicate the time lapse between the question and the answer. If necessary ask for time to consider a question before responding. Remember that your deposition testimony will only be heard in court if it is read word for word. Make sure your responses are phrased to satisfy that eventuality.

5. Be positive. Avoid qualifying words and phrases unless they are absolutely essential to your answers. The unnecessary use of such terminology as "more or less," "I guess," "possibly," and "sometimes" dilute the effectiveness of an answer and are an invitation to the opposition for further exploration.

6. Listen to your client attorney. Objections by your counsel may be made during your deposition. Stop talking and pay attention. The objection probably contains a message for you, for example, that a question is improper, or that a question has been asked and answered.

   The first objection tells you that the question can be misinterpreted, and you should seek clarification. The second is a message that the opposition may have found a weakness in your testimony and is seeking to force a contradiction. You will usually be allowed to answer after the objection, and your response should consider your attorney input.

7. Maintain concentration. After a series of questions requiring carefully thought out responses, you may get a series of "easy" technical questions that appear to have obvious answers. There is a tendency to relax under these conditions with potentially unfortunate results.

   There are no unimportant questions. If some seem trivial, assume that they are a prelude to a forced response to an important question. Rather than resting between hard questions, visualize where the opposition is trying to lead you. Be sure to word "easy" answers so that conceded possibilities cannot be turned into probabilities by your adversaries. Never let down your guard.

8. Correct mistakes. If it occurs to you during your deposition that a previous answer was in error or might need clarification, request the opportunity to address that question again. If the opposition refuses

(which is unlikely) your own counsel will give you that opportunity later.

9. Be careful of leading or misdirecting preambles to questions. If a question starts with the phrase "Well, you will certainly agree that . . . " or words to that effect, it is almost certain that you won't agree.

   The question that starts "Oh, one last question . . . " is usually not an afterthought, but an attempt to cause you to relax and be off guard. It is likely the most critical question you will be asked. Think long and carefully before you respond to "trappy" questions.

Things to Avoid

1. Don't guess. You cannot be expected to know everything there is to know about your area of expertise without reference. If you don't know an answer, say so. If it is something you intend to look into later, say that too.

2. Don't cast your position in concrete. Don't state that your mind is made up, and no circumstances could cause you to reconsider. Base your opinions on existing information, but don't express fixed judgments that more detailed investigation might undermine. Reserve the option to do further investigation if you decide it is appropriate.

3. Don't argue. Opposing counsel may try to draw you into an argument in order to get emotional rather than considered responses. Argument is a lawyer's strength. Don't play his game. You can usually terminate an argument with the statement "that is my professional opinion." If the response elicits a sarcastic response, ignore it. It means you have won the argument by default.

4. Don't be facetious. All participants in legal processes from the time of the incident to the end of the trial consider the events to be very serious. Attempts at humor almost always fail, and serve only to diminish your stature. If you feel the need for comic relief, save any witticisms for the recesses, and then choose your audience with discretion.

5. Don't talk about the case during breaks in the process. If opposing counsel initiates a social discussion during a recess, talk about nothing, the weather, or the local ball club. Offer no general personal or professional information about your activities inside or outside the case. Don't discuss the case in public places, even with your own attorney. You don't know who bystanders might be, and what information will get back to your opponents.

6. Don't offer gratuitous information. Don't answer questions that have not been asked. Don't qualify an answer beyond what is absolutely necessary to maintain its accuracy. This advice is redundant to what has already been offered as "things to do." It is repeated here because it is of paramount importance. Remember that depositions are largely "fishing trips" for the opposition. Don't take the bait.

7. Don't let the opposition put words in your mouth. If opposing counsel starts a question with "What you're saying is . . . " that is probably not what you are saying. Don't respond with a "yes." Answer the question in its entirety again for the record using your own words. Remember that the use of semantics to obscure meaning is a legal skill.

The foregoing suggestions are not absolutes. They are general guidelines, not firm prescriptions for witness behavior. If you learn and follow them, you will usually avoid any pitfalls from which your own counsel cannot rescue you after the adversarial interrogation.

Sometimes the "rules" appear to conflict. You cannot, for example, always avoid the use of the word "possibly" and at the same time avoid taking an unalterable stand. You must decide in real time which rule is more important at any given instant. In the final analysis, your own intelligence, judgment, and intuition will determine how closely to adhere to these "rules," and when to depart from them in the interests of improving your position.

IT'S STARTING TIME

You now have a thorough understanding of your opinions, and the evidence and technology upon which they are based. You now know the opposition strategy in deposing you. You now understand the tactics you can use to defend your position.

Despite all of this preparation, you are probably nervous about the upcoming experience. You are not alone. Many actors feel stage fright before the first performance of a new play, as do many professional athletes before the start of each game.

You are effectively in the same position before each deposition or trial. The opponents are new to you, the setting is strange, and the script is unwritten. Nervousness is not all bad. It gets the adrenalin flowing and keeps you alert as the proceedings start. Once the deposition is under way, the concentration needed to participate effectively will dispel any anxiety. The deposition is no ordeal if you are properly prepared.

CHAPTER 9

The Deposition

"If thou art a person that hast good authority with the company, 'twere good to look confidently, yet not scornfully, and then mildly say 'This is my opinion'."

—Thomas Fuller,
Introductio ad Prudentiam

THE BACKGROUND AND THE SETTING

Your deposition usually takes place in the offices of either of the attorneys, or in the offices of a court reporting service. As a matter of good practice, don't be deposed in your own home or office. That can only provide the opposition with ideas for inquiry, or requests for readily available materials to which they are not entitled.

The deposition setting is informal compared to a courtroom, but evidence developed there has, in theory, the same weight as testimony given in court. Attorneys for both sides as well as a certified court reporter will be present. Where there are multiple defendants, they will usually each be represented by counsel and each defendant may also have a company representative present. In some jurisdictions opposing experts may also be present at the deposition.

Examination during a deposition may appear more intimidating than what you will experience in court. During a trial you will be examined first by your own counsel, and given the opportunity to present your qualifications and your opinions in a favorable manner. Only then will you be subject to hostile examination. During a deposition, the proceedings effectively start with cross-examination.

A good opposing attorney can elicit your testimony in a manner which might appear to you to weaken your credentials and distort your opinions. Don't let it disturb you. Stay calm, stay alert, and answer all the questions carefully and truthfully. If you err in your responses, your counsel should give you the opportunity to clarify your position before the end of the deposition. Remember that if the case is tried, the agenda will be more to your liking.

THE DEPOSITION STARTS

The court reporter will swear you in, and the atmosphere will go from jovial to somewhat tense. From now on anything you say is under oath. The first questions are easy, and the opposing counsel asking them is probably being affable and trying to help you relax. Don't.

Anything you say on the record may be read to a jury in court. Anticipating this possibility, some lawyers will start a question with the phrase "will you tell the jury" even though no jury is present. Your words, even to your own counsel, off the record, or during recesses can give your opponents ideas for questions they might not otherwise ask. Be careful what you say at all times until you are well away from the deposition site.

The specific questions asked and the order in which they are asked depends on the judgment and preferences of the deposing attorney. They may come in any order, but most attorneys proceed logically somewhat as follows. After you have given your name and address, the formal deposition process usually starts with easy questions.

Q. *My name is Bill Williams, and I represent the XYZ Manufacturing Company. They are one of the defendants in the lawsuit you're here to testify about. You've been identified by the plaintiff as an expert witness to give some opinions you have about the accident that occurred at the Anytown Steel Company on January 11, 1999. We're here to find out about those opinions.*

I'm going to assume that you understand any question I ask. If not, let me know and I'll restate or explain the question so that there is no misunderstanding. Now, please tell me about your education.

You should have a copy of your curriculum vitae in your file. Rather than relying on your memory, read the education section exactly as it is written. Since your time at deposition is usually paid for by opposing counsel, you will probably be interrupted by opposing counsel.

Q. *Is that document you're reading from a C. V.?*

A. *Yes.*

Q. *May I see it? Let's mark this as an exhibit and save time. (Exhibit marked for identification by the court reporter).*

Q. *Does this document accurately represent your educational and work background?*

A. *Yes.*

Q. *Is the document current or is there something you want to add or change?*

A. *The document is current.*

With your C.V. entered in evidence as an attachment to your deposition, expect some questioning about the details of most of the entries. The questions may start from your education forward, or from your present employment backward. It's a little easier to maintain continuity of thought working from past to present, so many attorneys will question you from present to past. Remember, in court you get to tell it as you prefer. The questions are still easy to answer, but they begin to get a little more personal.

Q. *What is your present employment?*

Q. *What do you do in that job?*

Q. *What did you do in your previous job?*

Q. *Why did you leave your previous job?*

Q. *What about the job before that?*

Q. *Were you ever fired?*

Q. *Were you ever charged with a crime?*

Q. *Did you graduate from college with honors?*

Q. *Have you ever received any formal training in robotics?*

Q. *What courses did you take that make you an expert in this case?*

Q. *How does your job experience qualify you as an expert on industrial robots?*

Q. *Have you ever designed a robot?*

Q. *Have you ever designed a part that went into a robot?*

You can be an expert on robots even if you never saw one before. You may have experience with other machinery driven by similar power sources, using similar hydraulic or pneumatic actuators, having comparable gear drives, and using like control systems. Bring this out in your responses.

Next may come a series of questions designed to show bias on your part in favor of your client.

Q. *How many court cases have you been involved in as an expert witness?*

Q. *How many times have you been deposed?*

Q. *What percentage of your income last year was from work involving litigation?*

Q. *What percentage of your work is for plaintiffs (or defendants)?*

Q. *How many cases have you worked on for the lawyers employing you in this case?*

Q. *What is your fee for this type of work?*

Q. *What is your fee (or salary) for work not related to litigation?*

Answer truthfully, and don't be apologetic. If the case is tried, this approach to discrediting your testimony will not be very effective if your credentials are in good order and you testimony is credibly presented.

TURNING UP THE HEAT

Now the opposing lawyer will attempt to discover all of your opinions, and will try to fix them so that you cannot easily alter them before trial. If your opinions are set, opposing experts can then devote a major part of their efforts to finding flaws in them. If you keep some options open, the opposition can't be certain of what might happen. The questioning may proceed as follows.

Q. *What opinions have you developed in this case?*

Q. *When did you first form opinion number one?*

Q. *What is the basis for that opinion?*

Q. *What documents did you use in arriving at it?*

Q. *When did you form opinion number two?*

Q. *On what do you base that opinion?*

Q. *Is there any other reasonable scenario that would explain what happened?*

Q. *What about this possibility (other scenario described)?*

Q. *Are you confident that your opinions are valid within the limits of scientific probability?*

Q. *Is there anything that might cause you to change your mind?*

You should have clearly defined all of your pertinent opinions in your own mind before the deposition so that you are able to state them succinctly, completely, and without hesitation. Only state opinions that bear on the legal basis of the case, but do not omit any valid germane opinions. Your client attorney may or may not use them all in trial, but by stating them all you keep them available. On the other hand, don't be a nit-picker. If you find fault where very little (or none) exists, you run the risk of appearing unreasonable and biased.

If your opponents have some undeniable scenario favorable to their position, admit its possibility, but don't endorse it. Acknowledge what you must, but reserve the right to think about its credibility and change your mind. Don't ever deny the obvious. But note that this is a good place to deviate from the "be positive" rule of Chapter 8.

When acknowledging a scenario advantageous to your opponents, words like "sometimes," "maybe," and "possibly," along with phrases like "I'd have to think about that and do some research" are useful to allow you time to time to evaluate its effect and its probability relative to your own scenario. On the other hand, if you have already thought of the enemy scenario and discarded it with reason, feel free to say "I don't consider that a reasonable possibility."

Your opinions probably developed gradually as you became more familiar with the case. You may have had some original "first look" impressions, but these were not firm opinions. Be clear in differentiating between them if you are asked. Avoid the appearance of prejudging the evidence.

I once had a luncheon discussion with a highly respected professor of electrical engineering who visited my employer laboratory as a representative of the National Bureau of Standards. His assignment was to review test data we had developed on a product whose manufacturer was contesting a Bureau ruling. Our testing was peripheral to the main area of dispute, and our results were neutral, favoring neither side.

During lunch, and before showing him the test results I asked what he expected to find. His response as nearly as I can recall was "the product is no good, it never was any good, and it never will be any good." So much for impartiality. I suspect that this bias was evident at a subsequent trial, because the courts eventually found for the manufacturer.

Finally, to this set of questions, if you were not certain of your opinions within the limits of scientific probability, you shouldn't be expressing them in a deposition, so the answer is "yes." And you might change your mind, but only if new and convincing evidence were presented. However, you don't expect this to happen.

NOW FOR THE DETAILS

Somewhere during the questioning, probably after you state each opinion and the reasoning behind it, the opposition will inquire into specific factors affecting that opinion. The depth and duration of this questioning probably varies directly with the complexity of the case and the impact of your testimony, and inversely with the skill of the attorneys.

If the opposition attorneys know where they are going, they can find out quickly what your opinions and their possible impact are. If not, the deposition may turn into a fishing expedition. I have been deposed in periods ranging from two hours in some cases to several days in others. Typically a deposition will last from three to six hours.

The search for details may include questions along the following lines.

Q. *Is it your opinion that any of the defendants violated any industry or government standards in this case?*

Q. *Which standards do you believe were violated?*

Q. *In what respect were they violated?*

Q. *Did Mr. Doe observe the operator precautions listed in the standard?*

If you are certain that accepted standards effective at the time of manufacture of the equipment were violated, cite chapter and verse. If you are not certain, but feel there may be a violation, indicate that the product violates "good commercial practice," and may well violate some standards. Further state that this is an area you intend to investigate.

With regard to Mr. Doe's actions, a defense expert might opine that Mr. Doe violated a standard by standing in the wrong place, failing to use a safety belt, bypassing safety devices, or by some other deviation from good operator practice.

A plaintiff's expert might opine that most standards are prepared by manufacturer dominated groups, that the operator never gets to see the standard, that common practice in the industry is to operate the way Mr. Doe did, and that all the manufacturers know that and should allow for it in their design.

Paradoxically, both experts may be correct and truthful in these responses. It remains for the courts to decide which of these truths is more important in any particular case.

Q. *What tests did you perform on the robot?*

Q. *How fast did the robot move just prior to the accident?*

Q. *How did you determine that?*

Q. *What is the margin of error in your estimate?*

Q. *How much notice did Mr. Doe have that the robot was malfunctioning?*

Q. *How do you know that?*

Q. *Is that enough time for Mr. Doe to have taken any action for his own safety?*

These are typical probing questions about what you did in your case research and testing. The answers are fixed by the data, and will show no weakness if you did your homework well. Your function here is to report your work effort in a confident manner without editorial comment.

Good opposition counsel usually will not show any emotion if they sense weakness in your approach. They will accept what you say with the intent of saving any disagreement for court. You may be amazed at how pleasant and receptive they are to your testimony now. Remember that they are just biding their time.

On the rare occasion when a deposing attorney becomes belligerent with the intent of intimidating you, become as polite as possible. A satisfactory answer for the record might be "I'm sorry that my testimony seems to upset you, but that is my opinion." If the verbal attack comes in the form of a comment, for example, "that sounds silly to me," don't respond at all, verbally or emotionally. Your sole purpose at a deposition is to answer questions, and this last remark is not one.

Next may come a series of questions exploring the technical basis for your opinions. This is a particularly good place to observe the chapter eight "do" and "don't" rules.

Q. *Tell me again why you think the widget caused the robot to malfunction.*

Q. *Why do you consider the material unsuitable?*

Q. *What materials would be better?*

Q. *What are these pictures and charts?*

Q. *Explain what this chart means.*

Q. *What does this photograph show you that affects your opinion?*

Q. *What do these X rays mean?*

Q. *What should the manufacturer have done to prevent this accident from happening?*

This line of questioning is routine and may be repetitive. A fundamental axiom of effective cross-examination for attorneys in court is not to ask a question unless they know the answer. Much of what you are being asked is to assess the probabilities of winning in court, and thus the merit of pretrial settlement. But some of it is to fix your answers if the case is tried and you are subject to cross-examination.

Again your answers should be exactly what you have developed during your preparation for the deposition. The only question that may require an ambivalent answer is "what should the manufacturer have done?" Except where the defect is a glaring departure from good practice, your response should avoid detailed information on how you would remedy the defect.

It is enough to state that the widget design and materials should have provided adequate strength with a safety factor sufficient to prevent failure. Do not suggest how to redesign the widget. That is something you could do if you were hired by the manufacturer, and given sufficient time.

You may be asked what the safety factor ought to be. Again do not be tied down to a specific number. The number might be two or might be ten. You would have to review the entire robot design to pick a number, and that would be an extensive project. Don't hesitate to protect your position with a statement to that effect. You don't have to carry a technical library in your head. If some point requires further investigation, say so.

INTERLUDE

During the deposition there will be some stressful moments as you strive to develop the most cogent possible response to questions you may not have anticipated. You wish there were time to gather your thoughts. On occasion there will be. Lawyers get into legal discussions, usually starting with an objection by your counsel. This may seem an ideal time to review your thinking, but wait for the legal interplay to develop before you do.

The "do" rules of Chapter 8 say pay close attention when the attorneys argue about the complexities of a question after an objection. There is an exception. At times attorneys in their wisdom will argue among themselves, and the debate may become protracted. The discussion may be legal, personal, or both. The following abstract from a deposition transcript exemplifies what may occasionally happen.

Lawyer A   *And your experience is that they hire people who speculate and say things that aren't founded on good scientific principles?*

Lawyer B   *Object to the form of the question.*

Witness   *If you're asking me if I think your expert is speculating, the answer is yes.*

Lawyer A   *That is not what I'm asking you. Read my question back to the witness. (The question is read back).*

Lawyer B   *There is no question pending.*

Witness   *I—*

Lawyer B   *Don't say anything. There is no question pending.*

Lawyer A   *Of course there is a question pending.*

Lawyer B   *There is no question pending. That—*

Lawyer A   *What is wrong with you? He had it read back to him.*

Lawyer B   *So she read the question back. He didn't say: would you please answer the question.*

Lawyer A   *Do you understand the question as read back to you, sir?*

Lawyer B   *That is exactly the point. There was no question pending.*

Lawyer A   *You remember the question?*
  to Witness

Witness   *I think I do.*

Lawyer A   *You want it read back again?*

Witness   *Not unless (Lawyer B) thinks it is necessary.*

Lawyer B   *I want to know if there is a question pending. If you are asking him to—she can read the testimony all day long. If you are asking him: Would you please answer the question, do you understand the question, that is fine.*

Lawyer A   *I tell you what, why don't you ask the questions that you want when you get your chance to ask questions and let me ask the questions that I want. And you can object to my questions or you can instruct the witness not to answer the questions. But let me ask my questions, and I will let you ask your questions.*

Lawyer B   *That is fine. There wasn't any question you asked.*

Lawyer A   *He was ready to answer the question before you started arguing about whether or not a question existed. All I'm saying is let him answer the question if he understands it. All right?*

Lawyer B   *If there is a question pending, I will.*

Lawyer A   *Do you remember the question?*
to Witness

Witness   *I think I do.*

Lawyer A   *Now she's ready.*

Witness   *My answer is . . . (witness answers question).*

Somewhere early in this debate it becomes obvious that no important communication from the client attorney will be lost by thinking about something other than what the lawyers are saying. At this point the opportunity exists to think comparably to a computer running two programs simultaneously, one in the foreground and one in the background.

Keep an ear tuned to the proceedings as they occur, but take the opportunity to think about what the opposition strategy is, what you have said up to this time, and what answers need clarification. You may ask to clarify a previous answer. If the deposing lawyer says no, your own counsel will ask you the question on cross-examination.

Also take the opportunity to rest your mind in preparation for the resumption of hostilities. You can always ask for a physical break in the deposition procedure if you feel the need, but use any hiatus in the interplay between the opposing counsel and yourself to good advantage. It's amazing what a minute or two of mental stress relief can do to clarify your thinking.

WINDING DOWN

Once the opposition attorneys are satisfied that they have all of the critical information they are likely to get from you, a series of "easier" questions are used to tie up loose ends and cover anything that may have been missed previously. There is a tendency to relax at this point.

Don't! As Yogi Berra said, "It ain't over till it's over." Stay alert and continue to observe the "do and don't" rules of Chapter 8.

Q. *Have you discussed the technical aspects of this case with any other experts?*

Q. *Have you read the reports or testimony of other experts prior to forming your opinions?*

Q. *Do you have any opinions about this case that we have not addressed?*

Q. *Do you intend to do any further work on this case prior to trial?*

The first two questions are matters of fact requiring "yes" or "no" answers. A "no" answer will terminate that line of questioning, and is usually the truthful answer. A "yes" will invite further inquiry, but again the responses are matters of fact and easily constructed.

The final two questions are important. A "no" answer to these questions may make inadmissible at trial any new opinions you may form, or the results of any new research you may do. Answer these questions in a manner to keep your options open.

Suitable replies include "I don't have any other opinions at this time, but I'm still thinking about it and may develop some," "I may do some further testing to confirm my opinions," and "I may build some models or displays to help a jury understand my theories." The response will usually be "If you do any of these things, let me know through your attorney. I reserve the right to redepose you to discover any new information you may have."

THE DEPOSITION ENDS

When opposition counsel says "That's all the questions I have," you can relax a little, but not completely. It's now time for your attorney to help you correct any inaccurate impressions you may have given, or to engage in damage control if you made any significant errors. You may take it as a compliment if your counsel says "I have no questions."

If your attorney asks a question for the record, try to understand the implication of the question. It will be based on something you said or didn't say during the deposition that affects the weight of your testimony. There may be some clue in the wording of the question that will help you understand the problem.

When you understand the point counsel is making, respond truthfully, but choose your words carefully to rectify any possible previous misunderstanding. When your counsel says "I have no further questions" and when opposing counsel says "I'm finished," you can finally afford mental relaxation. Just remember the Chapter 8 rules about maintaining a serious demeanor, and avoiding gratuitous case-related comment at the deposition site.

Finally, you will be asked if you want to read and sign the transcript of the deposition. You should always get a copy of your deposition for your own later study. If you are certain that you made no errors, and that no transcription errors can be significant, you may waive the right to sign.

If the deposition is at all lengthy or complex, exercise your right to read and sign (in a notarized statement). This gives you the opportunity to correct any transcription errors, and to correct any erroneous statements you may have made. It is difficult to justify amending a statement made while being deposed, but it is less harmful now than if faced with altering your testimony at trial.

Now comes trial preparation. Discuss the time and cost with your attorney client. It may be that a settlement will obviate the need for further work. When the client says "go," start developing a courtroom presentation that can best communicate your opinions to a jury. The next chapter offers some thoughts on how to do that.

CHAPTER 10

Exhibits and Demonstrations

"We talk far too much. We should talk less and draw more. I personally should like to . . . communicate everything I have to say by way of sketches."

—Goethe,
Attrib.

COMMUNICATION BY DEMONSTRATIVE EVIDENCE

A principal function of an expert at trial is to make a technical concept comprehensible in a very short time to nontechnical people. You're expert at what you do. Your training and experience in your area of expertise makes the body of knowledge on which you rely seem to you easily understood. It's probably not. Don't underestimate the difficulty of conveying your theories to others outside your profession.

It is not enough to say in effect "I am an expert, I know these things to be true, take my word for it." You must make it as easy as possible for lay persons to understand what you did, why you did it, what it meant, and how you were able to arrive at the opinions that you hold. Demonstrative evidence is a most powerful tool for this purpose.

The general definition of demonstrative evidence is something that supplies information to the senses before anything is said about it. This would include anything from a power drill in an electrocution case to a document in a breach of contract case. Note that this type of evidence is not probative. It proves nothing unless it is supported by appropriate testimony.

The definition used here is more limited. It embodies only evidence in the form of illustrative or visual aid that is introduced for the sole purpose of clarifying the verbal testimony of an expert. This includes, but is not limited to, photographs, X rays, photomicrographs, thermographs, charts, computer simulations, computer graphics, videotapes, models, and courtroom demonstrations.

It is accepted by the educational community that most of what we learn comes from what we see and do, rather than from what we hear. Memory of visual experience is also considerably better than that of purely auditory experience. Properly selected and used, exhibits and demonstrations are very effective. Conversely, if they are poorly conceived, they can lose the attention of an audience, and on occasion, a case.

Once introduced as evidence, a visual exhibit can be left in place during an attorney's entire presentation, thus developing a lasting impression in the mind of a jury. The exhibit then accompanies the jury to the jury room where it serves as a constant reminder of whatever salient point it was intended to support.

A visual exhibit does not have to be complex to work well. One of the most effective exhibits I have ever seen was used by defense counsel in a case involving an injured maintenance worker. It stood on display during much of the defense presentation. It was simply a poster board citing in large print the plaintiff's own words immediately after the incident, "That was stupid of me, I should have known better."

Courtroom exhibits should be professional. Making exhibits for courtroom use is a task better left to skilled crafts personnel. Nevertheless, the exhibits are your product, your responsibility, support your opinions, and must be made under your direction and supervision to be used effectively in court.

The propriety of an exhibit also assumes that it meets certain legal standards. A proper foundation should exist, i.e., an exhibit should adequately address the issue in question. It should meet the Frye standard of scientifically accepted theory. It should be relevant. It should explain something important to the jurors that they might not understand without it. It should not mislead the jury. And it should not be prejudicial or inflammatory.

These standards are not absolutes, and the use of some exhibits becomes a fit subject for judicial discretion. Getting court permission to use your exhibits is the responsibility of your client attorney. Be sure to keep the client informed of what you are doing in this area. And be sure that there is enough time for the opposition to see and question the significance of an exhibit before trial, so that the claim of surprise evidence cannot be raised to suppress it in court.

TIMING AND THE MESSAGE

Jury duty includes periods of intense boredom. Jurors are required to listen to much that serves the legal system, but does not impact directly on the decisions they must make. The tempo of their thinking is tightly controlled by the presentation of the attorneys. Exhibits thus become welcome interludes to the jurors, dissipating tedium and allowing them to think at their own pace.

There is an important corollary. The typical juror will immediately start looking at an exhibit, attempting to decipher its meaning before it is explained. This concentration may be enough to distract from your verbal testimony. There are two "rules" that should be observed to minimize this effect.

First, do not show any exhibit until you are ready to discuss its meaning. If the exhibit is too large to move, keep it covered until you are ready to display it. Second, keep the exhibits uncomplicated. Each exhibit should, if possible, make only one salient point. Don't tempt the jury to try to anticipate from part of an exhibit what you might intend to say later about something else.

PHOTOGRAPHS

Photography has been described previously as a primary tool in case investigation. You should have a large relevant collection of your own photographs at this stage of a case, as well as copies of those offered by your opponents at deposition. If you used enough film while investigating, some of these will be of high enough quality to serve as a basis for courtroom exhibits.

Having selected those photographs that meet that standard, several alternative means of display are available. Enlargements are mandatory, but the degree and method of enlargement depend on the proposed method of presentation.

The most common method of showing a photograph to a jury is to use an enlargement that is clear from a reasonable courtroom distance. This means enlargement to poster size, typically twenty by thirty inches, mounted on rigid backing. This size permits the use of an easel and pointer to explain the significant features to all of the jurors simultaneously.

The same degree of enlargement can be accomplished with a slide or overhead projector, but these have some significant drawbacks. First is the potential for equipment failure during your presentation. Second is the possible need to dim the light in the courtroom to improve visibility. Third is the difficulty of reorienting the display for better viewing.

Any of these events will distract observers and detract from your presentation. When you can avoid the use of electrical and mechanical devices in your presentation, do so. Play the percentages and go with hard copy when you can.

A less common technique for displaying photographic evidence is to use smaller enlargements, typically eight by ten inches, and to show these to the jurors individually. This technique is more difficult to implement, but does afford person-to-person contact with the jury while conveying your message.

A last alternative is the handing of the photograph to the jury, and allowing it to be passed from one juror to another. Although I have seen this method used, I fail to see any particular merit in it. The choice of methods to be used will depend on the attorney's preferred trial tactics, and should be discussed with your client before starting the preparation of exhibits.

CHARTS AND GRAPHS

These exhibits follow the guidelines for photographic exhibits with a few additions. They should be professionally crafted, but should avoid giving the impression that they have been created by an advertising agency. They should be as clear and uncomplicated as possible. They should address one major point of evidence at a time. They should, as much as possible, distill the essence of your testimony into simple and irrefutable logic.

With regard to craftsmanship, the lettering and line work should be done by competent drafting persons. The use of bright contrasting colors to convey information may be used, but should not be overdone. Size should be adequate to convey information clearly to the court, but should not be so large as to be overwhelming.

Sometimes the number of ideas to be addressed by charts is so large that the use of an individual chart for each thought becomes awkward. A good alternative exists in the gradual display of diverse material in a single exhibit. A chart may contain a number of salient points that are sequential, and can be effectively grouped once each point is explained. There are at least two satisfactory ways to deal with this.

First is concealing various parts of the exhibit with easily removed opaque material until you are ready to discuss the hidden information. Second is the use of transparent overlays that add new ideas to the exhibit as they are put in place. My own feeling is that this latter method is a little too pretentious to inspire confidence, but it is a matter of personal taste. I have seen both techniques used effectively.

Graphs are useful for displaying complex numerical relationships in a comprehensible fashion, but they can be misleading. Huff,[18] in the book *How to Lie with Statistics*, describes the "Gee-Whiz" graph which aims at misrepresentation.

Two graphs are used to represent growth in payroll with time. Both graphs have an identical linear horizontal axis expressing time in months. The vertical axis, also linear, expresses payroll in dollars. The first graph shows full-scale vertical values from nineteen to twenty one million dollars, and the second graph shows full-scale vertical values from zero to thirty million dollars.

Payroll rose over a six-month period by less than 4 percent. The first graph showed growth in payroll to be represented by an almost vertical line, and was misleadingly entitled "Payroll Up!" The second more truthfully showed growth to be an almost horizontal line entitled "Payroll Stable!"

Avoid graphical exhibits which deceive. They will either be barred by the court, or exposed and explained by your opposition in a manner which will make your exhibit appear to be an attempt to mislead.

Much high technology analytical instrumentation provides output in the form of computer generated graphs, or oscillograph traces. These may be converted photographically to appropriately sized exhibits, or may be reproduced by graphic artists. Photo reproduction is preferable to avoid challenge, but artistic reproduction allows editing to simplify and clarify.

The way you plan to present this type of data is worth considering while the information is being generated. Try to keep original instrumental output as clean and presentable as possible. Don't make notes or observations on the original. If you must select only certain areas of a graph or plot for display, be certain that you have a credible explanation of why those areas were selected, and why other areas were not important.

VIDEO EXHIBITS

The ready availability of good video cameras, recorders, and monitors makes video presentation an easy, cost-effective, and exciting way to arouse juror interest in your testimony. The admissibility of videotape to document and relay information is generally accepted by the courts.

The Federal Rules of Evidence categorize videotapes with photographs. Most jurisdictions accept that definition, and the rules for admissibility are similar to those for photographs. If a video picture is relevant, if it accurately shows what it is supposed to show, and if it is more probative than prejudicial, it will probably be admitted.

People are accustomed to learning from television news, documentary, and educational programming. This tends to create a subconscious confidence that what is seen on television represents the truth. Some courts struggle a little with this phenomenon, but usually allow the use of video at trial.

The courts reason that people also tend to believe what they hear from prestigious and persuasive experts. These experts are not prevented from testifying, and by the same token video evidence should not be barred. Thus, a powerful communication tool is available to you. In addition to being an easy way to bring your audience up to speed in your presentation, it may have positive subliminal impact. Use it whenever it can be effective.

A videotape of an accident scene must be done essentially under the conditions that existed at the time of the accident if the tape is to be relevant. However, the inclusion or exclusion of audio is usually an expert decision. If background noise or your own statements on tape play a role in your scenario, record the audio. If you want a silent tape so that you can dub in audio testimony or talk live during its playing in court, don't record the sound.

The audio portion of a videotape can record your off-camera remarks. Even though the tape is edited for court, your opponents are entitled to an uncut version of the tape for their study after your deposition. Be careful of what you say during taping, and produce a tape that will require as little editing as possible.

If you have no experience with field video work, you have two ready alternatives. First, you can subcontract the work to a professional. This has the disadvantage of requiring real-time discussion between you and the camera operator, with the dialogue usually being partially recorded on the tape.

Second you can acquire video equipment for a modest investment, and develop an interesting peripheral skill for your litigation work. My own experience is that using the camera yourself is preferable. You can record all that you want to, only what you want to, and with less possibility of omitting important material. The results will usually be at least as good as that of most field camera operators, and more satisfying.

The text *How to Use Video in Litigation*, by Buchanan and Bos,[6] is a definitive work covering both the legal and technical aspects of the preparation of video evidence. Written primarily for lawyers, it describes a number of considerations germane to effective courtroom video presentation. If you doubt your own skill and creativity, you may want to read this book before making a "build or buy" decision.

COMPUTER ANIMATION

A special category of video evidence is computer-generated animation. Requiring professional programming and considerable computer power, it is costly to produce and is thus not used as often as might be helpful. It has two main applications. First, it can be used as a tutorial to help explain scientific or technical principles. Second, it can be used to reconstruct an incident according to the theory of the most probable scenario.

In both cases the presentation stands or falls as admissible evidence based on the expert testimony it accompanies. If the expert testimony is admissible, any tape that helps the jury understand the reasoning behind the testimony will probably be allowed as evidence.

The explanation of scientific principle can involve something as basic as Newton's laws or the operation of simple hydraulic systems. Or it can explain something as intricate as nuclear powered ion propulsion from the viewpoint of the proverbial "rocket scientist," or the construction of the eye as understood by an ophthalmologist.

In some cases commercial animations of general scientific principles can be obtained from government, educational, public service, and industrial groups. Check this availability before creating your own computer demonstrations.

A reconstruction of an accident by means of computer-generated animation is very convincing, even to the expert who sets the parameters. Computer imaging can provide views of an accident from any of a number of different angles, and can provide a jury with a clear understanding of how much real time was involved in each event leading up to an accident.

This time factor is particularly important if the "last clear chance" doctrine is being invoked. There is a vast difference in effect between being told that a person had two full seconds to react to avoid an accident, and seeing how short a time that is when two vehicles are about to collide.

The quality of computer simulation for courtroom exhibits should be somewhere between the crude graphic displays of early versions of Microsoft's "Flight Simulator" and the overwhelming graphics of *Star Wars*. A good standard of quality can be found in a short promotional videotape[15] available to prospective purchasers of computer generated animation for forensic purposes.

This video shows the last minutes of a real life fatal aircraft accident, from the time the plane taxied into position on the runway until the crash a minute later into a building. Panoramic views are shown of the scene to provide orientation, followed by a view from the cockpit with the altimeter reading prominently displayed.

The video is synchronized with an audio recording of the actual tower to aircraft communication just prior to and during the incident. The sensation of sitting in the pilot's seat, and listening to the real developing panic of the crew as the crash approaches is enormously persuasive.

MODELS

Modeling fills much the same niche in courtroom exhibition as does computer animation. Lacking the momentary impact of videotape, both static and working models have merits not present in video display. Primary among these are the facts that they are always visible during jury deliberation, and that they may be handled by the jury, appealing to the sense of touch.

There are three substantially different modeling techniques for supporting technical testimony. The first of these is miniaturization, or the use of a scale model to depict an object or area too large for introduction into a courtroom. I tend to avoid miniaturized models. The objective of persuasion can be better reached, in my opinion, by the use of photographs, charts, or videotapes to convey the same information.

A second model type is an enlarged model of a small object that is difficult or impossible for a jury to examine in detail. These models are usually "working" to the extent that they can be disassembled to show individual parts during testimony as to their function. One of the best examples of this that I have ever seen is a model of the human eye with a linear enlargement of about fifteen to one.

That model could be manually disassembled to show the cornea, the iris, the pupil, the lens, the optic nerve, and other associated parts. The model was extremely well designed and finished. The parts could be handled and examined, giving an impression of instant familiarity. The workings of a mechanism as complex as a human eye could be understood by a lay person in a matter of minutes rather than hours.

After witnessing a comparable demonstration on computer animated videotape, I had no doubt that the model was superior as a medium in this case. A satisfactory generalization is that video animation is preferable where a sense of motion must be conveyed, while modeling is more effective where a concept is static and requires repetitive examination to grasp.

A third type of model is a working subassembly of those parts of a mechanism to which the expert attributes failure. I once had the need to explain to a jury how an industrial vehicle with its shift lever in neutral could suddenly shift into forward with no operator on board. The vehicle had a fairly complicated powershift transmission which would be difficult to explain.

Because I believed the problem lay in the transmission control valve forward-reverse spool, I designed a cutaway working model of the valve mechanism only, using the manufacturer's parts except for the cutaway housing. A full-scale model about eight inches long and weighing a few ounces was thus used to explain to a jury how an accident occurred in a five ton vehicle fifteen feet long.

The model forced the jury to concentrate on the simple area in question rather than becoming involved with the entire transmission. They were able to move the valve spool in the housing and observe the less than positive locking action of the valve assembly. I feel the model played an important part in the jury's understanding and eventual favorable decision.

Models that allow jurors to become active participants rather than passive observers can provide technical instruction to a jury without undue effort. Moreover, active participation by jurors increases their interest in your testimony. If you can get the jury's attention, and if you have credible evidence to present, your testimony will be productive. Good working models help. Use them whenever they seem appropriate.

DEMONSTRATIONS

Live demonstration or experimentation at trial is probably the most effective of all the methods of persuading a jury. And the most dangerous. Murphy's law says "Anything that can go wrong, will go wrong." A logical addendum for the courtroom says "Don't fool around with Murphy."

Any live demonstration that fails is a major plus for your opponents. If there is any possibility of failure, forget about doing it. Don't take a chance unless you are absolutely certain that your demonstration will work every time you try it. And make sure that nothing happens between your final testing of the exhibit and trial to affect what you want to show. Consider the following examples.

A quick release latch was used to maintain the integrity of some scaffolding. The latch released when a dropped hammer accidentally hit it, and the structure partially collapsed. The release of the latch under impact was found to be characteristic of the design.

An exemplar latch was procured and set up in a fixture as a courtroom display. Before trial, it was struck lightly a number of times with a hammer, and it released every time. The repeated testing apparently deformed the latch enough to eventually prevent its release under impact. When the demonstration was used in court, the latch failed to "fail." The exhibit became a prime piece of evidence for the opposition.

In another case I was using a high pressure high capacity hydrogen valve as an exhibit. It was my intention to gradually disassemble the unit in court while I explained its operation. The disassembly was to start by removing a single retaining bolt. When it left my possession, this bolt was only finger tight, and could be easily removed.

The night before the trial, and for no particular reason, I asked to see the exhibits. The valve was in the courtroom where it had been introduced as evidence by another witness. I reached over casually to loosen the key bolt by hand, and nothing happened. Using a twelve inch crescent wrench also had no effect. It took a heavy duty box wrench, a handle extension, and a hammer to loosen that bolt.

I have no idea how the bolt became tightened. I was too preoccupied with testimony the next day to look for any strange reaction from the opposition when the valve easily came apart. I do know that failure to disassemble the valve would have seriously impaired my credibility. I checked that exhibit before trial only by chance. Since then I check all exhibits just before trial by design.

Videotaping demonstrations has some merit. Both of these demonstrations could have been done with more assurance on videotape, although that would have prevented person to person contact with the jury. Another consideration mandating the use of video for a demonstration is the physical safety of the court.

An electric paint sprayer was alleged to have caused a fire while spraying a flammable lacquer. The sprayer contained an open brush type motor which sparked visibly. I felt that the spark energy was too low to cause ignition, and verified that opinion by laboratory testing in a small chamber containing an explosive lacquer-air mixture.

Working with another engineer, we decided to perform a full-scale experiment to simulate the conditions under which the fire started. An outdoor room was framed and covered with transparent plastic. The sprayer was activated and allowed to spray lacquer from a small drum for some time without causing a fire. I was sure, within the limits of scientific probability, that the sprayer was safe. But not with scientific certainty. My associate was both more certain and more brave.

Wearing a mask, he entered the room and manually operated the spray gun for a period of time while being videotaped. After he left the room, the lacquer-air mixture was ignited by a coil and spark plug. The results were spectacular. Shortly after the tape was shown to the opposition, the case was settled favorably.

IN SUMMARY

The reader interested in knowing more about the techniques of preparing and using exhibits for legal purposes should study the *Demonstrative Evidence Sourcebook*[13]. This volume describes in detail the technology, technique, preparation, presentation, and the economics of courtroom exhibits.

The psychological effects on juries of exhibits, their composition and the methods of presentation are detailed by Hamlin[16] in the text, *What Makes Juries Listen*. Written primarily for attorneys, this document offers some interesting insights into the good and bad mental reactions stimulated by various types of exhibits.

Incidentally, Hamlin also offers some advice to attorneys on the psychological handling of technical experts. The book may tell you more than you want to know about that subject, but it does provide interesting material for reflection and speculation.

In the final analysis, the preparation of good demonstrative evidence is not complex. Common sense, professional workmanship, and careful association of what you show with what you intend to say, will assure that your exhibits serve their intended purpose well.

CHAPTER 11

Before the Trial

"In all things, success depends upon previous preparation. And without such preparation there is sure to be failure."

—Confucius,
Analects

IT'S HOMEWORK TIME

A case in which you have been named as an expert witness seems about to come to trial. You've done your case investigation, developed your scenario, prepared your exhibits, and given your deposition. No problem. Well, maybe one problem.

It's been a while, perhaps a year or more, since you last thought about this case. Since then other witnesses have been deposed, new evidence has been produced, and the case has an imminent calendar date before a specific judge and court. Moreover some of the defendants may have been dropped from the suit or have settled the claims against them, thus altering the case for both the plaintiff and the remaining defendants.

Meanwhile, you've been involved in a number of other projects, and your recollection of this case is vague. Now is the time to start studying as if for a competitive final examination which will be graded only win or lose.

You may literally have a number of file drawers full of correspondence, statements, complaints, interrogatories, answers, reports, depositions, photographs, videotapes, exhibits, and other items pertaining to this single case. You don't remember everything in there, and even if you did, you wouldn't haul it all to court with you.

Start by going through the files, and examining every item in them. Put aside anything that is clearly irrelevant to your impending testimony, and organize the remainder in logical order. Review carefully each remaining item to assure that the information is either pertinent to your presentation, or may be needed during cross-examination or rebuttal testimony. Again set aside anything that appears superfluous.

You may still retain a formidable amount of documentation, but it is all pertinent, and probably condensed to manageable size. It's what you are going to use for final case preparation. And you had better be more familiar with it than anyone else in the courtroom.

PREPARE YOUR ATTACK

During the proceedings up to now you may have come up with a number of justifiable complaints, or a number of good defenses. Your client may elect to disregard some of these for strategy reasons. Consult with the client before starting your final preparation to make sure that you are preparing to testify only on the issues that will be tried.

Outline your most probable scenario in a series of sequential and concise statements. Next describe the cause or causes of the incident based on your best judgment. You should be able to do this in less than two hundred words. If you can't, rework your thoughts to prepare the most succinct summary possible. Keep this summary in front of you as you review all of the evidence.

Now reread every document and deposition in your files, making notes of the location (page and line number) of each piece of evidence that supports your theory and each piece of evidence that opposes it. Pay particular attention to the depositions of opposing experts, and be prepared to point out flaws in their procedures or in their reasoning.

Save your own deposition for last, and identify what statements you intend to emphasize in court, and what statements you may have to defend under cross-examination. Know exactly what you said and why. It's easier than it sounds. You'll be surprised at how well you can recall your testimony as you read the transcript. Remember that most of the assault on your credibility will come from opposition study of that document.

At trial your direct testimony will start with a series of questions from your client attorney, probably followed by the question "Will you explain to the jury why . . . ?" This permits you to address the jury directly with your explanation of the facts. Be prepared to do that well, for winning or losing can depend on how well you communicate.

Organize your presentation the way you feel will be most effective, and try it out on audio- or videotape, or in front of a mirror. Try to make it clear and unequivocal. The courts are overworked, and the jurors are taking time from their everyday lives to perform a public service. Your obligation to them is to convey your testimony in a clear, concise, and accurate manner. Go over the organization and content of your testimony until you are satisfied that you can. The court will appreciate it.

PREPARE YOUR DEFENSE

Your position, established by direct examination, is going to be attacked under cross-examination. How you defend yourself may have more effect on the jury than your direct testimony. Favorable evidence presented under cross-examination carries extra import because it is obviously unrehearsed.

By now you know generally what technical theories will be used to counter your position. You don't know exactly what questions the opposition will ask, or how the questions will be phrased. Time that you spend in trying to predict a few key questions and developing good answers may prove the most valuable part of your case preparation.

Cross-examination is usually limited to questioning about your direct testimony, but don't count on that. You may be required to testify outside that scope under any of several legal theories. Concentrate expressly on anything you said during your deposition, particularly if you have had reason to amend your testimony since then.

Prepare a list of questions that you would ask if you were on the opposite side of the case, and prepare the best answers that you can. Select from that list those questions that have the most advantageous answers, and form a shorter list of questions that you hope you are asked. Work and rework answers to your "hope" list until you are convinced that your response has maximum impact. If you are lucky enough to be asked one of those questions, the answer may confound your opponents.

I once testified in a case involving a chemical plant equipment fire which resulted in one fatality. The applicable codes in effect at the time the equipment was installed did not address the fire hazard problem, although later versions of the codes did. The equipment and procedures involved did conform with these later versions of the code. When I made this observation during direct examination, an objection was made and upheld that the ex post facto code was not relevant. The jury was instructed to disregard that testimony.

Under cross-examination I was asked if it might not have been better to observe a different safety procedure which could have prevented the fatality. It was a question on my "hope" list. I pointed out that the alternate procedure would have certainly caused the explosion of a nearby hydrogen storage facility, would surely have leveled the entire plant, and probably would have caused a number of fatalities. The jury agreed with that analysis.

Once you're satisfied with your presentation, it's time to review your thoughts face-to-face with your client. This should happen with enough time before the trial to allow you to refine your presentation. On occasion this isn't feasible, and you may find yourself in the first definitive client discussion about your testimony just before you are to be called as a witness.

Avoid this situation if you can. If you can't, be sure that the preparation on your own part was conceived and implemented to the best of your ability. Absent personal contact with the client, use the telephone frequently to confirm that you are both heading in the same direction.

CONSULT WITH COUNSEL

You and your client have a mutual teaching and learning responsibility. The attorney should instruct you about the remaining legal issues, and about how the law is interpreted in the jurisdiction where the case is to be tried. You should be sure the attorney understands exactly what your testimony means as well as what it doesn't mean. Neither of you should overestimate what the other understands. A communication breakdown at trial often produces unfortunate results.

Counsel should be able to provide you with a summary of tentative questions that will enable you to develop your opinions on direct examination. Along with that you should get a feeling for the types of questions to expect under cross-examination.

You might want to amend your answers to both types of questions from the standpoint of presentation, but obviously not from the standpoint of truth. For example, if called on to explain the relationship between electrical voltage and current, you can do it truthfully in two minutes by analogy to water flow, or equally truthfully in two hours by teaching basic electricity.

The depth of response desired is probably somewhere in between, and depends on attorney trial tactics. The attorney should review your tentative answers to assure that they respond to the questions and that they adequately inform the jury, but that they are not so comprehensive that the jury will lose interest or understanding.

Review with counsel the case file you intend to take to court. You want everything in it that supports your position, material that you intend to enter as evidence, and anything you may want to use to help you on anticipated cross-examination. You want the file arranged and indexed so that you can find anything in it quickly and without fumbling. What you don't want in that file is extraneous material that does not bear on your testimony.

I watched a case in which a competent expert seriously injured his credibility by bringing superfluous material to court. The opposing counsel asked, and was permitted to review all of the material in the witness case file during a recess. He noticed an envelope of site photographs bearing a later date than the last occasion on which the witness testified that he had visited the scene. Counsel returned the file without comment.

During cross-examination the witness reaffirmed that he had made no recent visits to the scene. Opposing counsel again asked, this time in front of the jury, to examine the file. He pulled out the envelope of dated pictures, handed them to the witness, and asked him to explain the date and content.

I believe the witness had made an honest mistake in dates. Nevertheless when asked by opposing counsel "Did you just forgot about that visit?" the apparent confusion weakened all of the testimony of the expert. It undoubtedly played some part in the jury verdict.

Finally, review with counsel all of your exhibits and demonstrations to make sure that they are still relevant to your final presentation. Be absolutely certain that nothing can go wrong in their use. If they are dependent on technical support facilities such as video gear or overhead projectors, be sure that counsel will have the best possible equipment available in court and in good working condition. Try to have redundant standby facilities available on a quick reaction basis just in case.

REVISIT THE SITE—VISIT THE COURTROOM

With help from your attorney you may occasionally be able to visit the site of the incident in dispute one last time before trial. Looking again at the scene of an accident that you have investigated is a powerful mnemonic tool. It's worth the effort. If you get the chance, take it.

Again with the assistance of counsel, visit the courtroom where the case is to be tried. Pick a time when the court is not in session so that you can move about freely. Observe the layout of the courtroom with particular attention to the spatial relationships that will exist between the judge, the jury, both counsel, and yourself.

Determine where to place exhibits and perform demonstrations so that they can be clearly seen by judge and jury. Visualize how you will explain the exhibits or perform the demonstrations without interfering with the view of the judge or any of the jurors. I have been reminded by judges on several occasions that blocking a juror's view of a television screen while explaining the picture was not good practice.

Check any facilities that are a part of the courtroom, and that you intend to use. Among other things, this might include electrical outlets, light switches, window blinds, sound systems, and chalkboards. If the courtroom lacks any facilities you will need, make sure that they will be available from some source at the time of your appearance.

SOMETHING ABOUT JUDGES

Judges occupy a special place in society. Underpaid by the standards of the legal profession, they are compensated in part by the prestige, respect, and power that accompanies the title "Your Honor." Judges usually deserve and are always entitled to the highest degree of respect. Be sure to observe that protocol.

Judges "preside" in the fullest sense of the word. As the chief officers of the courts, they govern, moderate, control, and direct the proceedings according to their own preferences. There is no higher authority while the court is in session. And there are as many differences between judges in their operating methods as there are between any other professionals.

If a judge has predilections in the way cases are tried and testimony is presented, it's worth knowing about them ahead of time. Your client attorney should be able provide you with guidance as to what pleases and what irritates the judge who will preside as you testify. "Pleases" is better than "irritates."

Good judges think logically, act fairly, and maintain their own decorum as well as that of the other participants in the trial. They manage time well, and move trials apace while providing a reasonable opportunity for both sides to present their arguments.

Ideally, the judge is a moderator rather than a participant in the search for civil justice. On the other hand the judge can exert a substantial influence, positive or negative, on the jury's perception of an expert witness. My own experience is that a judge will usually protect an expert from badgering by the opposition if the witness offers reasonable testimony. Consider the following abstract from a trial record.

Opposing Counsel	*Please, in order to save time, I would prefer it if you would answer the question "yes" or "no." Please do so. If you need to explain your answer, feel free to do it. But if the question is susceptible to "yes" or "no," I would appreciate it.*
Client Counsel	*Your Honor, I object to instructing the witness how to answer the question. If he wants to explain the answer, he is certainly entitled to do it.*
Judge	*It doesn't appear this witness is the evasive type we sometimes get. He is entitled to answer it his way. I don't think he has to answer it "yes" or "no." I realize sometimes we instruct the witnesses to do that if they are getting too far out of line. Go ahead and answer your own way.*

You can probably count on a judge who will be fair if you observe the amenities of the courtroom and provide credible information. There is of course no guarantee. Only once, early in my career, did I testify before an obviously hostile judge who took an active part in the direct examination.

I was testifying as to the proper means of inspecting an industrial freezer refrigeration coil which had failed resulting in substantial consequential damages. The coil bore the Underwriters Laboratories seal of approval. The testimony, as I recall it, went something like this.

Judge   *Do you mean to tell me that you have to inspect that coil even if it has the Underwriters seal on it?*

Witness   *Yes, Your Honor.*

Judge   *(disdainfully) I don't believe it.*

I was so surprised that all I could think of at the moment was to shrug my shoulders. In retrospect I should have responded that Underwriters Laboratories gives type approval to designs, and does not test production units. I should have pointed to the light fixtures in the courtroom ceiling and the switches on the wall, and observed that they too had the Underwriters seal.

Finally I should have said (respectfully) that Underwriters Laboratories never saw those fixtures and switches, and they never saw that coil which carried their seal. Unfortunately I couldn't go back and make that point, but I have been waiting over thirty years for it to happen again. So far it hasn't, but if it ever does I'll be ready.

SOMETHING ABOUT JURIES

"In suits at common law, where the value in controversy shall exceed twenty dollars, the right of trial by jury shall be preserved, and no fact tried by jury, shall be otherwise reexamined in any Court of the United States, than according to the rules of the common law." So said the Seventh Amendment to the Constitution of the United States in 1791. Some two hundred years later the system is still working, usually quite well.

Jury selection is both science and art on the part of attorneys. The law wants an impartial jury. The lawyers don't. As part of the adversary system of justice, lawyers do their best through peremptory challenges and challenges for cause to seat a jury they feel will favor their side of a case. If opposing counsel are equally skilled at the voir dire, the jury picked will be reasonably impartial.

A good jury from the viewpoint of an attorney may not be the easiest jury to inform about technical issues. Attorneys are concerned with sympathy, empathy, and predisposition of jurors to favor one side of a case or the other. You prefer jurors whose background permits them to follow and evaluate your presentation without confusion, but who do not have enough knowledge of your specialty to play the devil's advocate. That's a role for an opposing expert.

Jurors with some knowledge of the technical issues in question are usually willing and able to convince the rest of the jurors that their own evaluation of the technical testimony is correct. This is particularly true if the person expressing the opinion has had supervisory responsibility. Whether or not an attorney wants someone like that on a jury depends on personal judgement, and to some extent on the verdict sought.

Contrary to a common belief among attorneys, many skilled workers have little sympathy for others with the same skills who are hurt at their work. Most electricians, mechanics, machinists, and construction workers with whom I have discussed cases involving their trades have a common reaction. "It's their own fault. I wouldn't do that. If it happened to me I wouldn't expect to be paid for it."

I'm not a professional educator, and I have been known to confuse people at times with my explanations. My own preference is to have at least one influential juror with enough background and training to understand what I am trying to say, but not enough to try to guess what I am going to say.

I would, for example, rather explain hydraulic system operation and malfunction to a high school mathematics teacher than to a hydraulic specialist. The teacher will be interested in learning what I have to say. The hydraulic specialist will sit in the role of a critic with established conceptions and misconceptions. If there are any ambiguities in the testimony, they will certainly be misconstrued by the specialist, and become an important issue for discussion during jury deliberation.

Regardless of the makeup of the jury, it's important to know the education, orientation, and skills of the various jurors. This allows you to express your thoughts and form analogies in a manner to which the jurors can relate. Your client should make you aware of the jury makeup as soon as it is known.

Most lawyers accept the concept that no one can be sure of what a jury will do. There is some merit in this uncertainty in that it results in settlement of most cases, thus unburdening the legal system. Where discovery is complete and a case still appears headed for trial, the use of a focus group or mock jury can reduce the uncertainty, and furnish guidance on optimum presentation methods for both attorneys and expert witnesses.

The jury focus group is a tool developed by psychological testing organizations to provide attorneys with objective insight into how a jury will probably react to the evidence in a given case. It can also predict with a fair degree of probability what might increase or decrease the impact of that evidence. A scenario with which I am familiar goes somewhat as follows.

A seven person carefully selected "jury" listened to a presentation by a plaintiff's attorney of both sides of a case. The jury was kept unaware of whether the attorney represented the plaintiff or the defendant. The attorney presented the case for the plaintiff in fifteen or twenty minutes, followed by the case for the defense in the same amount of time. The jury then deliberated for two hours while the attorney listened.

The jury rendered a unanimous verdict for the defendant based on the fact that the plaintiff's case had not been "proved." This pointed up the need to stress that the level of proof was a "preponderance of the evidence" rather than "beyond a reasonable doubt." A second jury with that fact emphasized voted five to two in favor of the defendant. A third jury, with the presentation altered, voted four to three for the defendant.

All three of these "juries" indicated that they would have liked to hear directly from the "experts" before forming an opinion. When the case was tried two months later, the jury found unanimously for the plaintiff. This may have resulted from improved performance by the attorney as a result of focus group input, or it may be a commentary on the presentation of the expert testimony. In either event, the group input was useful.

Finally, treat a jury with respect. Don't make the cardinal mistake of underestimating the intelligence of the jury as a whole. A jury brings to its deliberations the combined knowledge and life experience of a number of people, most of whom take their responsibility to the court very seriously.

It's safest to assume that as a group they are at least as smart as you are, and at least as perceptive. They are just less informed than you in your particular area of specialization. If you think and act otherwise, you may be fooling yourself, but probably not the jury.

For the reader seeking more insight into the selection and functioning of juries, suggested reading is Blue's[4] *Jury Selection—Strategy and Science*, Wenke's[41] *The Art of Selecting a Jury*, and Joiner's[21] *Civil Justice and the Jury*.

THE DIE IS CAST

Your preparations are complete, and trial is ready to start. Some few cases are still settled just before trial, during the voir dire, or even during the early stages of testimony. Much more likely, any case that has gone this far will be tried and the decision left to the courts.

There is every reason to believe at this point that your opponents have as strong a belief in their side of the case as you do in yours. They will certainly have experts in your field who disagree with you. But if you have done the best that you can in preparation, you need have no concern about the outcome. Most trials are won by the side that did the best preparation. In any case it's too late to worry. It's show time.

CHAPTER 12

The Trial—Part One

"A trial is still an ordeal by battle. For the broadsword there is weight of evidence; for the battle-axe, the force of logic; for the spear, the blazing gleam of truth; for the rapier, the quick and flashing knife of wit."

—Lloyd Paul Stryker,
Attrib.

SOME BASIC RULES

There are a few unwritten rules crucial to a successful effort as an expert witness in court. Observing them won't make a jury believe an unconvincing argument. Failure to observe them may cause a jury to be skeptical of what should be a winner.

Appearance

More than in almost any other type of scientific service activity, the first impression you give plays a key role in your success. Your total exposure time to the jury is limited. If you can spend that time reinforcing an initial favorable impression rather than dispelling an unfavorable one, your effectiveness will be greatly enhanced.

The judge wears a robe which lends authority and conceals whatever may be worn beneath. The attorneys, with some colorful exceptions, wear conservative garments suitable for any serious business situation. The jurors, in most instances, wear whatever they find comfortable, although shirt and shoes are required. Your own wardrobe should be in quiet good taste.

A dark well-tailored suit or suit-dress is a must. Shirts or blouses should be white. Accessories such as ties or jewelry should be conservative. Shoes should be polished. Haircuts or styling should be recent, neat, and in accordance with community standards. What might be appropriate in New York City or Los Angeles may not be suitable for a rural setting. Assess the community from which the jury will be drawn, and dress to meet those standards.

Demeanor

Be especially careful of your behavior at all times when in or near the courthouse. You can never be sure of who is friendly to your opposition, or who may be a juror. Count on anything you say or do in hallways, elevators, restrooms, or even nearby streets and restaurants being observed by hostile eyes, and related to opposing counsel.

Jurors usually and rightfully take their responsibilities very seriously. Avoid any public display of humor, and by all means avoid any jesting in the courtroom. Anything other than a most serious demeanor is sure to detract from your credibility. While on rare occasions there will be laughter in the courtroom, it should always be spontaneous rather than contrived.

Confidence

Perhaps the most difficult task of the expert witness is to give an initial impression of quiet confidence when, in fact, there is always some emotional turmoil upon entering a courtroom as a witness. For most people, including myself, the initial apprehension is always there no matter how many trials they have experienced.

Once past the initial questioning by your own client attorney, adrenalin flow and concentration eliminate the stress, and any insecurity vanishes through total immersion in the proceedings. There are a few techniques which can help you get past this initial stage fright into the role of an active participant where you become unaware of your surroundings.

The first questions, involving factual information concerning your identity and background, will be asked by your own client, and should require little thought on your part. These are the icebreakers. Careful preparation of these questions and answers with your counsel before the trial gives you an easy start.

Practice your answers to these opening questions beforehand until you know exactly what you are going to say and how you are going to say it. Use a mirror or tape recorder to practice if you think it will help. While you're answering these "easy" questions without the need to concentrate, you can use the rest of your thought processes to become comfortable.

Orientation

From the instant you enter the courtroom be aware that you are communicating to the court whether or not you are speaking. Walk at a normal pace toward the witness stand. Speak in a normal tone of voice as you are being sworn in. Take the stand, and seat yourself comfortably.

If you have brought a file with you, take a few seconds to arrange the file so you can find anything you may need without fumbling. Incidentally, some attorneys prefer that you bring nothing with you to the stand because anything in the file may be examined by opposing counsel and placed in evidence if not previously entered. Now sit back and glance about the court quickly, but not furtively.

Look briefly at the jury box to identify the individual jurors. They will usually be instructed by the judge to remain poker-faced, and occasionally instructed to avoid eye contact. So don't be surprised if they're not looking back at you, or if they appear indifferent to your presence. You can be sure that they will observe you carefully when you're testifying.

Breath normally, and speak slightly slower than you ordinarily do. Anxiety tends to cause faster than normal breathing and speaking. If you consciously avoid the symptoms, you can also avoid the appearance of apprehension until it disappears. And it certainly will once you become involved in the complexities of the trial.

There are some other psychological techniques available to the expert still concerned with an initial attack of nerves. These include deep-breathing, tensing and relaxing muscles, mild fantasizing, and concentration on minutiae. The reader interested in further exploring these psychological aspects of stress relief while testifying as an expert witness is referred to the text by MacHovec,[25] *The Expert Witness Survival Manual.*

Body Language

Hamlin,[16] in the book *What Makes Juries Listen,* asserts that verbal communication in a native language requires only 15 percent of the brain to comprehend meaning, while body signals have no exact meaning (with a few notable exceptions), and require more concentration to interpret. Consequently she argues that body language is a more powerful tool of communication than speech. She may or may not be right. But there is no doubt that you had better look confident in the truth of what you are saying, or people won't believe you.

You are more persuasive if you maintain a "nothing-to-hide" posture. This means sitting comfortably with legs uncrossed and hands relaxed by your sides. Maintain good, but not excessive, eye contact with the person or persons you are addressing. Use your hands if you need them to describe something where words won't do. For example a large shaft, or even a shaft "six inches in diameter" is less communicative to a jury than a shaft "about this big," framed with the hands.

You can also use your hands to point for emphasis, but only at things, never at people. "That widget," or "that chart," or "that robot" with a pointing finger directs attention to where you want people to be looking when you make your next statement. Change the "that" to "the," don't point, and people will be looking at you when you speak. Pointing at people, on the other hand, is more aggressive than an unbiased expert ought to be.

There are a number of other body signals that are significant, for example posture, movement, and gesture which have both positive and negative aspects. The reader interested in an in-depth discussion of the pros and cons is referred to the chapter on nonverbal communication in the Hamlin text.

One-on-One

When you speak in the courtroom, you are theoretically not speaking for an audience. On direct examination you should be speaking only to your attorney. On cross-examination you should be speaking only to the opposing attorney. Your full attention should be on the person to whom you are talking. If you succeed in concentrating properly, you will soon be unaware of your surroundings or the other people present.

The jury is for the most part like an audience at a live show. Never talk directly to a jury. It is not your function, and most judges are protective of their juries. Turning and talking to a jury not only violates courtroom protocol, but risks a severe reprimand from the judge which will cast doubt on your integrity. There is one major exception.

Your client may want you to speak directly to the jury to enhance your credibility, or to establish a bond between the jurors and yourself. Counsel can ask the court's permission to have you step down and explain something to the jury by means of demonstrative evidence. Once permission is granted, as routinely occurs, you have the opportunity to persuade the jury directly of the correctness of your position.

Now you are able to establish eye contact with the jury. What you say, how you say it, and your body language, all become critical. You are on your own unless interrupted by your own attorney, by an opposition objection, or by the judge.

Stay focused on the information you are trying to convey. There is an innate tendency to explain everything you know about the whole case, including any reservations you may have. Fight it. Explain only what your lawyer has asked you to explain. Err on the side of brevity. If you leave out something important to the jury's understanding, your counsel can remind you with another question.

Speak to the jury on an equal plane. Avoid unnecessary technical language, convoluted explanations, and condescending speech. Speak clearly and unostentatiously. Talk normally as if you are helping a group of friends understand a simple concept, and they may well end up as friends for the purposes of arriving at a decision.

Closed Doors

There are some buzz words that you do not want to mention in your courtroom testimony. For example, the words "insurance" or "insurance company" from the witness stand are grounds for a retrial in some jurisdictions. In cases where some of a group of multiple defendants have settled before trial, reference to them may be barred by the court. You may also be prevented from referring to other similar accidents unless the court rules them admissible.

Alternately, if you do refer on direct examination to elements the court has ruled inadmissible for your opponents, you open the door to their exploration of areas that your counsel prefers remain unexplored.

Be sure to consult with counsel before trial on what subjects you should and should not address. Know what words should be considered out of bounds.

DIRECT EXAMINATION

Your client attorney is now going to lead you into giving your information in a manner most likely to persuade the jury that your side of the case is correct. The attorney acts as the director of an exhibition, talking to you directly at times, and asking you to address the jury at others.

The questions are designed to make life as easy for you as possible. Don't fight it. Don't agonize over your own counsel's questions unless there is a new and disturbing twist to them. You should be comfortable with the questions your own attorney is asking, since you have had a chance to review them and discuss answers ahead of time. There should be no doubt in the juror's minds that you and your attorney have mutual confidence.

The questions might go somewhat as follows. The answers should come easily from your memory, possibly enhanced by a copy of your curriculum vitae.

Q. *Would you please state to the jury your full name? (Now you can look directly at the jury).*

Q. *Where do you reside? (Now look at the attorney)*

Q. *Are you currently employed? (Look at the attorney while you answer).*

Q. *Why don't you give the jury a little bit of your educational background, please? (Look at the jury and tell them about your schooling).*

Q. *Did you do any graduate work? (Only asked if you did).*

Q. *After taking your degrees, what kind of employment or experience have you had, if you could just review that briefly for the jury? (Now you can talk to the jury at some length. Counsel may interject "reminder" questions such as "what was your position with that company?").*

Q. *What are your professional qualifications in addition to your education? (Talk directly to counsel about professional licensing and awards. If none, the question won't be asked).*

Q. *What professional societies or associations do you belong to?*

Q. *In the past what professional societies or associations have you belonged to?.*

Q. *What about publications in technical journals or government archives? (Asked only if there are some worth noting).*

Q. *What experience have you had with industrial robots and robot testing?*

Q. *Thank you. Let's go to your involvement with this particular case. Were you asked to review any materials or facts concerning this accident. (Answer to counsel: Yes).*

The party is over. You should have had enough time by now to get acclimated to your surroundings, and to be comfortable with the court and the jury. From here on your testimony will be more or less unrehearsed, and your mind must be in high gear until you are finally excused as a witness in the case. My own experience is that no conscious effort is required to stay alert, and mentally ready to meet any change in your attorney's agenda. The excitement of the moment provides all the stimulus necessary.

At this time opposing counsel may object that you are not qualified for whatever reason to testify as an expert on the particular item of equipment in question. The court will almost always overrule that objection, leaving it to the jury to decide how much of an expert you are and what weight to give to your testimony.

I once was called as a technical expert in a case involving a piece of conveyor machinery with which I had no previous experience. When the opposition objected on the grounds that I was not expert on that particular machine, my client attorney offered me as generally expert in rotating machinery. The court permitted my testimony on that basis. If you are at all qualified in your field, the chances of the court refusing to hear you are remote.

Q. Can you tell the jury what you reviewed? (Now you're talking to the jury again. Remember the admonition to focus your testimony on the specific question asked. For example, don't start talking now about what you found when describing what you reviewed. That comes later. Let your attorney set the pace).

Q. What else did you do in preparation for giving an opinion in this case and your testimony in this case? (Now you're talking to the attorney, not to the jury).

Explaining what you did may consume a considerable amount of time. It will cover all of your investigations, your interpretation of testimony from depositions, what you did on your site visits, your procurement of samples, your testing, your analysis of test results, and anything else you can think of except your opinions. If you overlooked anything, your attorney will ask a question to remind you of what you missed.

Q. Did you also examine the linkage between the control arm and the actuator on the robot?

Q. Did you do anything else in preparation for your testimony and opinion, or does that about cover it?

Now comes the crux of your testimony. There are two factors essential to establishing liability. The first is that a defect existed. The second is causation, i.e., that the defect was the proximate cause of the accident. If you are a witness for the plaintiff, your testimony should support both of those premises. If a witness for the defense, you should be prepared to offer an alternative more likely scenario. As an expert for the plaintiff the overall thrust of questioning might be condensed to the following three questions.

Q. *Based on the work you have done in this case do you have an opinion as to whether the industrial robot involved was defective or unreasonably dangerous?*

Q. *What is the nature of the defect?*

Q. *In your opinion how did the accident happen?*

In fact, the actual direct questioning may involve numerous more specific questions, the introduction of demonstrative evidence, and the consumption of hours of time. During the continuing direct examination remember the three basic questions above, and organize your interim thinking and responses to lead logically to the appropriate answers to those questions.

Objections and Side-bars

The smooth flow of your presentation will be interrupted more or less frequently by objections from opposing counsel. This tactic may be used as a serious objection to the legal admissibility of what you said or are apparently about to say. Or it may be a stratagem to cause you to lose concentration. Once an objection is made, stop talking and listen.

The most common objections to your direct testimony will be "irrelevant and immaterial," "assumes facts not in evidence," "hearsay," "no proper foundation," "leading the witness," and "calls for speculation." Later, on cross-examination, you may hear other objections by your own attorney such as "improper question," "argumentative," "asked and answered," and "not proper scope."

Sorting out the objections is a job for the attorneys and the judge. Sit quietly while they do it. Don't look at the jury and do pay attention to what the judge and lawyers are saying. After an objection the judge can either uphold it, overrule it, or ask the objecting lawyer to explain further. Once the judge rules, do not start talking until the lawyer questioning you poses a question.

Depending on the ruling, the question may be the last one asked or may take a totally new tack. During the discussion of the objection remember your train of thought just before your testimony was interrupted so that you can resume your testimony smoothly.

On occasion the basis for the objection or even the objection itself may not be considered legally appropriate for the jury to hear. Under these conditions the judge may ask both counsel to approach. Alternately, either attorney may request a side-bar with the words "Your honor, may we approach the bench?" At this time both attorneys and the court reporter will move to the judge's bench for a quiet discussion of the problem.

This process takes longer than open court discussion and may give you a good opportunity to lose your concentration. Don't take it. While the side-bar is taking place halt all your activities. Don't shuffle papers, examine evidence, or give any outward appearance that you are doing anything but waiting for the court to reach a decision. Look casually at the courtroom setting, sit calmly and quietly, and think hard about what you have been saying and what you want to say next.

The End of Direct

Your counsel will help you reach the end of your presentation with carefully conceived questions designed to present you and your opinions in the best possible light. You will have stated the reasons for the defect (or lack thereof), and you will have presented your most probable scenario of the accident cause. It is safe to assume that your scenario is favorable to your client, or you would not have been called as an expert witness.

Your client may punctuate your presentation with one hard-hitting question in summary of all of your testimony. "Is it your opinion that this accident would not have happened unless . . . ?" If you have done a good job of preparation and are satisfied that your testimony is the truth, you should be able to answer "absolutely," and your attorney should be able to say "no further questions."

The jury has heard everything you had to say about the accident. They realize that you have worked more or less as a team with counsel in making your presentation. They are inclined to believe you if you have done a reasonable job, but they certainly have some reservations about the full credibility of your testimony. They eagerly await your cross-examination to find out if you really knew what you were talking about.

Direct examination may at times appear contrived because it tends to follow a prearranged script. Cross-examination is perceived as the ultimate test of the truth of your testimony. It is unrehearsed, and its goal is to destroy your credibility.

If you do poorly, the jury will tend to doubt much of your testimony even though you have spoken nothing but the truth. If you do well they will give credence to most of the things you have said even if some of your conclusions border on speculation. This phenomenon was well characterized by Erlich[9] who wrote, "A clear-cut forceful answer given by a witness on cross-examination is more deadly in its effect on the jury than the same answer given on direct."

Cross-examination is the ultimate test of an expert witness, and you are about to face it.

CHAPTER 13

The Trial—Part Two

"In real life the witness's fortitude in the face of exposure (by cross-examination) is as remarkable as a human body's resistance to incredible torment"

—Louis Nizer,
My Life in Court

"Most trial lawyers perform with less skill and result during cross-examination than during other portions of the trial process . . . More cross-examinations are suicidal then homicidal"

—Peter Brown,
The Art of Questioning

THE EXPERT'S EDGE

The statement by Nizer is certainly hyperbole, and taken together with the statement by Brown, appears paradoxical. That's not necessarily so. There are substantial elements of truth in both quotations.

There is no way I know of to face cross-examination without some apprehension. About all you can do is be sure you know your subject and your recorded testimony better than anyone else in the courtroom. Follow the rules set forth for good response to direct examination. Hope that your opposition counsel is in the "suicidal" rather than the "homicidal" category. And remember that cross-examination is a two edged sword; your opponent is as liable to suffer damage as you are.

You do have some inherent advantages. First, the jurors usually hope you will do well. Most of them have undergone similar questioning during voir dire, and will sympathize with you. Moreover, you are effectively cast in the role of underdog, and rooting for the underdog is an American way of life.

Second, there are some self-imposed limitations on what a prudent attorney will ask. Except as a last resort, attorneys will only ask questions on cross-examination to which they are reasonably sure they know your answers. If they are wrong, a case can turn unfavorably for them on a single unexpected answer. Thus you can expect cross-examination to be based only on weaknesses in your previous testimony, and deposition testimony of opposing experts. You can pinpoint these factors in consultation with your own counsel, and be prepared to handle them in the most favorable way.

Lawyers will usually not try to argue with you in your own field of expertise, since that only provides you with the opportunity to reinforce the opinions you expressed on direct examination. Most attorneys realize their limitations in technical areas when competing with technical professionals, and limit their questions to peripheral areas.

I have known some engineers turned lawyer who try to use their technical skills during cross-examination to debate an expert. My own experience is that they do not excel at either profession, and should not cause the expert witness to be overly concerned.

Finally, remember that you know far more about your subject than the lawyer questioning you. Opposing counsel can only get guidance about difficult technical questioning from his own experts, and they cannot guarantee what your answers will be.

If your own attorney has planned well, your testimony will end both early in the day and early in the week. Thus the opposition counsel will not have the evening, or worse, the weekend to study your testimony before beginning cross-examination. Further, if you feel more alert in the morning or in the afternoon, your attorney may adjust his pace so that cross-examination starts at that time of day.

OPPOSITION STRATEGY

While you have been carefully establishing your position on direct examination, opposing attorneys have been watching, listening, and reviewing your previous deposition testimony with the sole purpose of discrediting you.

Don't take offense. It's part of their job description. If any of these attacks seems particularly severe, you may consider it a compliment. A basic principle of opposing counsel is don't waste time or risk harm by cross-examining in depth a witness whose testimony hasn't done much damage on direct examination.

Responding to cross-examination is probably the most pivotal activity of an expert in determining the outcome of a case. There are some standard lines of questioning and some useful response techniques which we will review here. For the reader who seeks a better understanding of the techniques of the questioner there are several good books available.

An excellent source for studying good and bad examples of cross-examination and response is Mulligan's[26] text, *Expert Witnesses: Direct and Cross-Examination*. Mulligan presents trial transcripts of seventeen experts, three of whom are non-medical scientists or engineers. The limited commentary accompanying the transcripts offers insight into winning and losing technique for both questioner and witness.

Other sources, less tutorial but equally interesting, are Wellman's[40] *The Art of Cross-Examination*, and Brown's[5] *The Art of Questioning*. Both of these describe anecdotally what is needed for proper questioning, but do not provide guidance on appropriate responses. Nevertheless the reader will gain some insight into what avenues cross-examiners will pursue and, equally important, what they will leave alone.

CROSS-EXAMINATION

Opposing counsel can take one or more of three basic approaches. They can attack your credibility. They can attack your testimony. Or they can attack your integrity. Whichever technique or combination is used, you can expect courtesy and no argument from any good attorney. Rudeness by an attorney questioning a polite, informed, and resolute witness is sure to put the jury on the side of the witness.

The attorney who considers your testimony arguable has two better options than debating with you in front of a jury. Opposition attorneys can use their own experts later to rebut your testimony, or can save the dispute for the closing argument to the jury when you can't answer back. Remember while you testify that your answers can be used in that way.

Attacking Credibility

Bias and incompetence are the two main parameters for impeaching an expert's credibility. The opposition almost always uses the expert's compensation as a means of establishing bias. The occasional exception is where opposition experts are more highly paid. Consider the following typical questions and answers.

Q. How much are you being paid for your work in this case?

A. My charge is one hundred dollars an hour for preparatory work, and one hundred and fifty dollars an hour for depositions and court testimony.

Q. How much time have you spent on this case up to now?

A. I don't know. Maybe two weeks.

Q. So you've been paid about ten thousand dollars or more?

A. Maybe. Or maybe less.

This testimony assumes you do not know the precise data requested. There is usually no reason to have exact figures available, and you are probably better off with an estimate. There is no way and no reason to conceal the fact that expert witnesses are paid well for their services.

Your own counsel can preempt the impact of this question line by asking you on direct examination whether or not you have a financial interest in the outcome of the case. You, of course, do not. The same question can be used on redirect, but appears more apologetic.

Your position must be that you are being paid for your experience, knowledge, and ability to think. Your testimony is coincidental to that, and you're not being paid for your testimony. Expert witnesses for both sides are paid, and that factor should be a wash in the jury's decision-making process.

Cross-examining counsel may try to create an impression of witness incompetence in the minds of the jury. That happened to me in a case where I was a consultant to plaintiff's counsel in defining a test program to determine whether or not to proceed with a suit. I suggested a screening test to determine whether a scenario favorable to the plaintiff was possible.

Failure of the test would prove the impossibility of the scenario, and warrant dropping the case. Passing would only show that the scenario was one of a number of possibilities, and indicate further work was in order. The test results were positive, warranting further testing. I declined to supervise that work myself because of scheduling problems, and the follow-on was carried out by others.

When the case came to trial, I was called as an expert primarily to describe the screening operation, and to lay a foundation for the testimony of the expert who succeeded me. The cross-examination went as follows.

Q. *The test that you ran didn't prove (the plaintiff's scenario) was correct, did it?*

A. *No, sir.*

Q. *So other tests had to be run?*

A. *Yes, sir.*

Q. *And you didn't run those tests. Someone else did. Correct?*

A. *Yes, sir.*

Q. *Now your role in this case was as a test engineer, was it not?*

A. *No, sir. My role was to advise counsel what to do next.*

Q. *Well the further testing wasn't done under your supervision as the expert test engineer, was it?*

A. *No, sir.*

Q. *Were you fired as the test engineer in this case?*

A. *No, sir.*

Q. *As the chief test engineer don't you think that if further testing was done they ought to have consulted you?*

A. *No, sir.*

Q. *Well that was your job, wasn't it?*

A. *No, sir. I told (counsel) that I was interested in lightening my work load. I would prefer to do only those things he couldn't find adequate help for elsewhere.*

The cross-examining attorney pursued this line of questioning for some time, eliciting the same type of response. There was no real reason for attacking my expertise because my testimony was primarily chronological, setting the stage for the battle between two experts who were yet to be called.

I had not testified on direct examination as to the relative merits of either the plaintiff's or the defendant's most probable scenario. To this point I had been relatively harmless, and it would probably have been a good place for the defense to discontinue cross-examination. Opposing counsel elected to pursue one other line of questioning aimed at eliciting expert testimony favorable to the defense.

Q. *Do your tests tell us that (the plaintiff's most probable scenario) is correct?*

A. *No, sir.*

Q. *In fact (the defendant's most probable scenario) is possible?*

A. *No, sir. In my opinion that's not possible.*

Q. *I read from your deposition dated. . . . . . Did I ask you these questions and did you give me these answers? (Reads Q. and A. where I had testified a year earlier that the defendant's scenario was a possibility).*

A. *That is correct. That is the answer I gave you at that time.*

It was obvious that I had changed my mind since the deposition. Opposing counsel didn't know why, and elected not to ask. After thumbing through the deposition for about a minute, cross-examination ended with "No further questions, your Honor." Plaintiff's counsel immediately picked up the ball on redirect examination.

Q. *You have apparently changed your mind since your deposition. Will you please tell the court why?*

A. *Since then I have had the opportunity to read two depositions, one by a defense expert and one . . .*

At this point defense objected on the grounds that those witnesses were to testify later, and their depositions were not in evidence. The court ruled that I could not say what was in those depositions, but that I could testify as to their effect on my opinions.

A. *Since then I read the depositions of an expert for the defense and an expert for the plaintiff. Based on the information in both of those depositions, it's my opinion that (the defense scenario) is not a reasonable possibility.*

Q. *No further questions.*

This line of cross-examination allowed me to inform the jury gratuitously that in my opinion the work of both experts who would testify later was more favorable to the plaintiff's case than to the defense. I don't know that this testimony helped the plaintiff's case. It certainly didn't hurt much since the jury ultimately found for the plaintiff.

If you are expert in your field, If you have prepared properly, if you have been truthful in your answers both at deposition and at trial, and if you stay alert, there is no reason to fear an attack on your credibility. Remain calm and polite in responding. The more aggressive opposing counsel becomes, the more polite you should be by contrast. You'll get a chance to hit back with some hard truth if the assault continues.

Attacking Testimony

There are three primary methods of attacking your testimony. The first involves leading you into fixed and awkward positions which later can be refuted by opposing experts, or which can be used against you without rebuttal in closing argument. The second involves improperly characterizing your testimony. The third involves using your deposition testimony to impeach you through your own apparent contradictions. If you stay alert, listen carefully, and respond appropriately, none of these methods or combination of them will do you any serious harm.

The "fixed and awkward position" technique is characterized by the following cross-examination. The case involved a machine in which two subassemblies made by two different manufacturers combined to cause a catastrophic failure. The original suit was against the machine manufacturer as well as the manufacturers of both subassemblies. And again my opinion as presented at deposition was favorable to the plaintiff.

Prior to trial the manufacturers of the machine and one of the subassemblies settled out of court. The case was tried solely to determine the negligence of the manufacturer of the second subassembly. During cross-examination some weakness in my own deposition testimony became apparent to me.

I had been questioned at length by counsel for each of the defendants during two depositions covering a three day period. The deposition transcript was over six hundred pages long, and it was difficult to recall on the stand everything that had been said. Counsel for the sole remaining defendant had questioned me at deposition partially as follows.

Q. *Was the control and timing mechanism between the two assemblies properly adjusted?*

A. *No, sir.*

Q. *Do you blame my client for that?*

A. *No.*

(further questioning, and then . . .)

Q. *Were all of the other components suitable for the application?*

A. *No, sir.*

Q. *Do you blame my client for that?*

A. *No, sir.*

This deposition questioning continued for some hours, and on several other occasions I did not "blame his client for that." Now the case was being tried solely on whether or not his client's component was a proximate cause of the accident, and I was being asked on cross-examination whether or not I blamed the sole remaining defendant for many of the factors surrounding the accident.

After responding "no" on three occasions I could see where this line of questioning was leading, and the nature of my mistake during deposition. The opposing attorney hoped to be able to say on closing argument "even their own expert doesn't blame us for the accident."

My repeated error at deposition was testifying as an expert in an area outside the scope of my expertise. The allocation of blame is not a technical judgment. It is an area for argument by attorneys and decisions by juries. I should have responded at the deposition as I ultimately did at trial. Soon after realizing what was happening at trial, I was asked once more.

Q. *Do you blame my client for that?*

A. *Sir, I'm an engineer. I'm not a lawyer and I don't know how you go about allocating blame. All I can tell you is that if the device built by your client was not defective, the accident wouldn't have happened.*

That was the last time I was asked that question. I may have answered "no" too many times before answering properly. The jury, originally divided down the middle, ultimately found for the defendant.

Based on post-trial discussion between attorneys and the jurors, I believe the jury would have found for the plaintiff against all of the defendants if two of the original defendants had not been "phantoms" at trial. In any case the verdict was not a disaster for the plaintiff. The pretrial settlement, resulting from the deposition testimony, was substantial.

Improper characterization of testimony is generally carried out at trial with a little sleight of hand. Be wary of any casual remarks from opposing counsel which do not call for a response. The following cross-examination demonstrates that style.

Q. *Let me show you an exploded parts drawing that you saw at your deposition. Did you draw those circles around those locknuts and initial them?*

A. *Yes, sir.*

Q. *Why?*

A. *Because you told me to.*

Q. *Were the nuts in place when you first inspected the assembly?*

A. *I don't know. I didn't have that drawing available.*

Q. *Were they there later when you saw it again.*

A. *No, sir.*

Now counsel is about to draw a conclusion for the witness which is not true, and which improperly characterizes the deposition testimony. The lawyer turns away and says as if to himself:

Q. *So that's one way the failure could have occurred.*

Don't concede anything just because it's easier to do that than to argue. Be hard to cross-examine.

A. *That was not my testimony. May I see that drawing again. Thank you . . . I testified that these cotter pins served exactly the same safety function as the lock nuts. As long as the cotter pins were inserted, that type of failure could not occur whether or not the lock nuts were present.*

Again, if you are honest, have prepared well, and remain alert, attacks on your testimony will go nowhere on the basis of improper characterization.

The final assault on your trial testimony comes from conflict with your own deposition testimony. If you have been deposed at length and if considerable time has passed since then, there are bound to be some discrepancies. You have no choice except to acknowledge them when they are brought to your attention, and to explain them in the best way possible.

The most common possibilities for discrepancy are change of opinion, testimony taken out of context, and error. We have previously seen that an opinion change warranted by new evidence presents no problem, and can in fact be beneficial. Changes in the absence of new evidence, or errors, are more difficult to explain without losing some credibility with the jury.

The only tenable position for that scenario is that you have thought about the facts a great deal since being deposed and, in the light of this further thinking, you have changed your opinions. This will certainly be attacked by the cross-examiner by asking "Are you going to change them again?" or "Who told you to change your testimony?" There is no question that your credibility is going to be hurt to some extent.

The harm will be less if you can respond that you stated during your deposition that your opinions were tentative and subject to change as you thought more about the problem. The down side of that coin is that your deposition testimony would have been weakened, and the chance of pretrial settlement decreased. You've made a mistake. It's a damage control situation. Do the best you can. Maybe it will be enough.

Don't hold still for opposition counsel trying to show conflict between your deposition and trial testimony by taking portions of your deposition testimony out of context.

Q. *Please read lines nine to fourteen on this page of your deposition (hands witness copy of deposition).*

A. *"I think that the handle may have moved from position one to position two due to vibration of the machine, thus causing the malfunction and the accident."*

Q. *Thank you. Now you've changed your mind?*

A. *No, sir. You will recall that I said I wasn't sure of that testimony and that I would verify it by test. I later ran a test proving that the handle did not move. I told you the results of that test, and gave you my final opinion in my redeposition last month.*

I believe that a lawyer who attempts to quote testimony out of context appears less than ethical to a jury, provided the witness is able to refute that tactic clearly with facts in evidence. The message here is know your deposition testimony well. Be alert for any attempt to change the meaning of your words, or to give them a significance they did not have. If it happens, speak up immediately in polite protest.

Attacking Integrity

A final ploy by opposing counsel is to attack the character or integrity of an adverse expert witness. It is generally not good "lawyering" technique, and carries a high risk of alienating a jury that may have previously developed a sympathetic feeling toward the witness.

In my opinion this approach is warranted under only two conditions. The first is where the witness has misrepresented under oath positive personal facts that can be refuted, or where the witness has deliberately omitted pertinent negative facts (e.g., failure to obtain a college degree that has been claimed, or suspension from practice due to improper professional conduct). It is assumed that the readers of this book do not fit either of these categories.

The second condition is that the witness has been very destructive to counsel's case, and that cross-examination has failed to shake the credibility or testimony of the witness. At this point opposing counsel may throw caution to the wind, and attack on a personal basis in the absence of any better alternative.

I recall only one instance of this technique in my personal experience. The purpose of the following examination was to make me appear a "bad guy" who was trying to win by ambushing the opposition. The opposing counsel started cross-examination with (simulated) great indignation. Taking the tack that my testimony was new to him, the questioning started:

Q. *All right, sir. Do you recall when you were kind enough to let me take your deposition?*

A. *I believe it was June twenty fourth of this year.*

Q. *Today is August the ninth, correct?*

A. *Yes, sir.*

Q. *And do you recall that at that time I asked you what all of your opinions were regarding any perceived defects or deficiencies in that machine?*

A. *Yes, sir, I remember that.*

Q. *Did you answer those questions fully and truthfully at that time?*

A. *I answered them fully and truthfully at that time, yes, sir.*

Q. *You understand, of course, that—you are an experienced expert witness in litigation matters, are you not?*

A. *I've been involved in a number of cases, yes, sir.*

Q. *And you understand the purpose of the Rules of Discovery and the deposition process, I assume. Is that correct?*

A. *Well I'm not an expert in that area, but I have some understanding of what it's for.*

Q. *Well when you submitted yourself for a deposition you knew, did you not, that I was very interested in learning anything you were going to say critical of my client's machine?*

A. *That is correct, sir.*

At this point counsel began itemizing all the problems I had found with the design of the machine on direct examination, and wanted to know why I had not told him all about them at deposition. In fact, prior to deposition the opposition had resisted the discovery process and failed to produce requested documentation until the day of the deposition.

I had no time to study those documents before being questioned. My deposition was based solely on material available to me up to that time, and that consisted of little more than the complaint and the "culprit" machine. At deposition I had responded to questioning as follows:

Q. *Can you tell me, sir, what you plan to do in the way of any additional work in this case?*

A. *I would suggest that we . . .*

I then detailed the work to be done to prove or disprove our initial theory. This new information was available to opposing counsel prior to trial, but he chose not to redepose me to determine its significance. The cross-examination continued.

Q. As I recall your, deposition, sir, you didn't have these criticisms at that time, is that correct?

A. Yes, sir. Because at that time I had asked you for drawings and materials specifications, and you had refused to let me see them. I told you then what I would do when I got those materials. And I've done what I said I would. Any opinions that seem strange to you are a result of what I did after you gave me the information that you were supposed to give me sooner.

This exchange stopped the personal integrity attack for the time being. Nevertheless, some apparently innocent questions were inserted during the remaining hours of cross-examination which were used to continue the integrity assault during closing argument when I was not in the courtroom.

I had built a demonstrative model of the failure mechanism of the machine using a cutaway housing which I had designed, and some fifteen parts supplied by the defendant. The following question was completely unexpected, seemed to have no bearing on the case, and caught me relaxed rather than wary.

Q. Did you build this? (holding up demonstrative model).

A. Yes.

In retrospect I should have said "Except for the housing, your client built it. All I did was assemble it." It was a classic example of getting caught off guard by the "Just one more question" disarming technique.

I had procured a number of parts from the manufacturer which were obviously hand-made to fit my very special order. I had testified to that fact on direct examination. Opposing counsel took my "yes" answer to the "model" question to elicit testimony from his own experts that anyone who could build that model could have built the "special" parts which I said had been received from his client.

I later learned that in his closing argument he postulated that I had built the hand-made hardware in order to make it seem that his client was involved in a cover-up. Justice was eventually served. The jury accepted my testimony and returned a favorable verdict.

Nevertheless, personal attack on your character is the most vicious type of cross-examination. If it is unwarranted, as it should be if you are testifying as an expert, it should not harm you. Find consolation in the fact that it may well be the last resort of a desperate lawyer.

THE REST OF THE TRIAL

While you were being cross-examined your own counsel has been noting any weaknesses in your testimony, any confusion about your position which has been created in the minds of the jurors, and any favorable testimony cut short by the opposition. Redirect examination (covering only facts brought up in cross-examination) gives you the opportunity to clear up these loose ends. Little or no redirect examination by your client attorney indicates that you handled cross-examination well.

You may now be subject to recross-examination by opposing counsel on matters discussed in redirect examination, but this is usually a matter of form rather than substance. Your part in the trial is over for all practical purposes.

Depending on the jurisdiction, you may or may not be allowed to stay in the courtroom after you have testified. Don't stay. Unless you are specifically requested to remain by your counsel, leave the courtroom as soon as possible maintaining the same degree of decorum you did when entering. Leave the building and the area promptly with no display of emotion. Just make sure your client can reach you on short notice if necessary.

I have never testified in a case where I was sure which way the decision would go when I left the witness stand. One way or another, you will probably hear the jury's verdict within a few days. You will experience a sense of satisfaction when they agree with you, and a sense of frustration when they don't.

In either case it's not necessarily a reflection of the jury's opinion of your testimony. I have known juries to find for a plaintiff where the only apparent reason was sympathy for the plaintiff. I have also known juries to find for the defendant where technical liability was clearly established, but where the defense doctor was more convincing than the plaintiff's doctor as to the extent of physical injury.

If you did your job to the best of your ability, you should be satisfied with either verdict. After all, clear-cut cases settle out of court. The purpose of judges and juries is to make the close calls. Paraphrasing the words of A. L. Williams,[42] "All you can do is all you can do, but (you're entitled to hope that) all you can do is enough."

CHAPTER 14

Business Development

"Never fear the want of business. A man who qualifies himself well for his calling never fails of employment."

—Thomas Jefferson,
Writings

STARTING A FORENSIC PRACTICE

Technical practice in support of litigation is a chain reaction. It's not easy to start. Once started, it develops its own momentum. The client community is vast in numbers and geography, but communication within the community is exceptionally good. Computerized data bases assure that success as a technical expert in a major case brought to trial will generate nationwide active interest for years thereafter.

How do you get started? You can, of course, join an organization specializing in forensic services (Appendix A). These companies will provide the necessary training and support to assure that your initial efforts are acceptable. This is not a viable option for technical personnel or organizations wishing to add forensic practice to their current activities. The intent here is to provide some guidance for this latter group.

The most certain way to start is by performing technical investigations for insurance claims offices. This approach has several advantages. First, there is a high demand for these services at almost all locations. Second, the local claims offices are more concerned with the facts essential to claims evaluation then they are with the courtroom experience of a potential expert witness. Third, you will usually have few time constraints and be under no pressure when carrying out the fact-finding mission.

You will probably gain a great deal of well paid experience in forensic technology without actively engaging in the litigation process. If claims are not settled, they are usually turned over to outside counsel who are either familiar with competent technical experts with trial experience, or who resort to the usual legal communications channels to find them.

Sooner or later, however, an attorney will read a report you wrote for an insurance company, interview you, and decide that you would make a good witness. From then on you're involved in the full litigation process. By then you should have enough exposure to forensics to handle yourself reasonably well under pressure. If you do well, you can expect further work from the same law firm, as well as from referrals.

Insurance companies show a preference for working with technical organizations rather than with individuals. If you are not affiliated with a technical service company or educational institution, you should probably form some affiliation, however loose, with one or more like-minded individuals for the initial marketing of your services.

Initial contact should be by direct mail in your local area, followed up by telephone calls seeking personal appointments. Some years ago I had the task of developing a forensic practice for a three person branch office of a company headquartered elsewhere. I prepared a form letter describing the local office capability, perhaps with a little too much enthusiasm, as follows.

If you're involved with liability claims, you must have information fast. Technically sound information. Hard facts. The kind that define and substantiate your position. We provide this data.

We specialize in technical claims investigation. We are staffed by technically oriented investigators. People with backgrounds in engineering and the sciences. Engineers who know what to look for. Whether in the lab or in the field.

Typical of the areas in which our experts have provided technical expertise are . . . (now followed a list of everything in which any of our people, including remote company personnel, had technical experience).

Telephone calls to some one hundred insurance company offices within a fifty mile radius (culled from telephone books) yielded the names and addresses of the appropriate people to receive the mailing. The mailing, again followed up by telephone calls, resulted in about twenty opportunities for personal visits. We ended up doing work for eight of the companies contacted.

Next we approached the independent insurance adjusters. The National Association of Independent Insurance Adjusters has local chapters in most metropolitan areas. These groups typically hold monthly dinner meetings, and are always receptive to volunteer speakers. I spoke at one of their meetings, showing a film of automotive crash testing with a little added commentary. As a result we acquired several more clients.

The volume of work from these clients over the next few years without further promotion was as much as that office was able to handle as a supplement to its normal business activities. If you have a specialty that is germane to accident investigation of any type, there is a market for your services if the client community is made aware of them.

Whether or not you proceed from the investigative stage to the litigation stage will be a matter of personal preference. If you have no desire to be an expert witness, you can maintain a good practice doing investigation without further involvement. However, the highest professional and financial rewards can be realized if you have enough confidence in your work and yourself to be willing to argue your position against other experts and hostile attorneys.

EXPANDING A PRACTICE

If you wish to develop a full forensic technical service more rapidly than happens by waiting for an attorney to find you, some direct sales effort is in order. Attorneys generally accept the curriculum vitae of potential experts as sufficient evidence of their technical skills. The primary concern of counsel is the ability of the expert to communicate opinions to a jury.

Only a personal interview can permit the lawyer to assess this factor. The sales effort should thus be directed toward developing face-to-face contact. There are two primary ways of developing the initial contact. First, you can meet with attorney groups in a semiprofessional setting. As with insurance adjusters, an offer to speak at a dinner meeting of the local bar association or trial lawyer group will usually be well received. Second, you can use direct mail.

The mailing should be limited to those firms of good reputation with trial practice in your areas of specialization. Although some firms represent both plaintiff's and defendants, most eventually become specialists for one side or the other because of potential conflicts of interest and the development of specialized skills. You should try to obtain business balanced between defense and plaintiff's firms to avoid the implication at trial that you only work one side of the aisle, and are therefore biased.

The best way to identify these firms is by referral. If you have been doing insurance investigative work, claims office personnel should be able to identify the major defense firms in your area. If you have developed any personal rapport with these people, they might also identify the major plaintiff's firms.

Alternately, you can contact the local lawyer referral organizations and bar groups. You can seek professional guidance from an experienced local lawyer who has no axe to grind. And finally, you can read the yellow pages, taking some of the advertisements you see with a little skepticism.

The mailing should contain a generalized curriculum vitae emphasizing those elements of your experience most pertinent to the specialties of the law firm. Later, engaged in the litigation process, you will probably shorten this document with emphasis on those things pertaining to a specific case.

ADVERTISING AND LISTINGS

Advertising and listing in professional publications is a useful medium if the personnel whose services are offered have some forensic experience in addition to technical expertise. For a start-up operation this would occur some time after initial success in the forensic environment.

Appendix A lists a number of publications, both local and national, suitable for professional advertising. Look through these at your local library to get a feeling for the nature and content of what constitutes an appropriate advertisement. Alternately, telephone or write the publication indicating your interest in advertising. Most publications will send you at no charge a media kit with rates and samples of their publication.

Advertising is probably more effective in selling the services of an organization than of an individual. Most attorneys whom I have known rely first on referrals either from their professional peers, or from data base information followed by lawyer to lawyer contact when trying to identify a good prospective witness. Second they will refer to a file of unsolicited letters containing the credentials of prospective experts. Third they will use an expert witness referral service. And only last will they attempt to find an expert for a particular case by reading advertisements.

Appendix A also lists a number of referral services specializing in finding expert witnesses for attorneys. Some of these are supported by attorney groups, some by experts, and some act as agencies for the technical expert. TASA (Technical Advisory Service for Attorneys), for example, will review your credentials before deciding whether or not to accept you for their listing.

Once you are accepted TASA will act as a prime contractor for your services, and you effectively become an independent subcontractor for the leads that it develops. You will have the opportunity to indicate your special capabilities by selecting from a list of over forty five hundred specialties in some thirty general areas of technical expertise.

TASA represents over fifteen thousand experts in these various disciplines. From my own experience, they are quite effective in developing forensic opportunities both locally and on a national level.

Another useful service for expert witnesses, which operates on a modest annual fee basis, is the National Forensic Center. The Center is supported by these expert witness annual fees, and prepares an annual directory of qualified personnel by category and location. The information is distributed in hard copy, and is also maintained on such data bases as Lexis and Westlaw.

This permits attorney access to the list from any location subscribing to these data base services. The ease of retrieval of the information may lead to "impulse" shopping. This listing service is inexpensive and warrants consideration in business development. The other referral services listed in the appendix may be equally effective, and are worth investigating.

BUSINESS CONSIDERATIONS

The success of any business depends on positive cash flow. Forensic technology is no exception. Before starting any project, you should have a clear understanding of how much, by whom, and when you are going to be paid.

Setting a Rate

First consider "how much." Remember that contingency payment is unethical (and in some states illegal) for an expert witness. The fee you establish must have some relationship to economic reality. You might start by asking knowledgeable associates what the prevailing rates are in your area for similar services. You might ask trial attorneys if you know them well enough to expect a truthful answer without causing resentment. Or you might want to refer to the *Guide to Experts' Fees*[27] for current information.

Some forensic service groups set fees lower than the prevailing rates in order to build sales. This may not work as well in selling intangible professional services as it does in selling commodities. I would hesitate long and hard before contracting with the lowest bidder for medical or legal assistance. This same concept applies, in my opinion, to technical experts who are to serve as witnesses.

Set your initial fees near the prevailing rate for competitive services in your area. You will probably find that they exceed the rates you normally charge for less demanding use of your capabilities. Charges can be set on an hourly rate or a daily rate. Many experts charge differently for depositions and courtroom testimony than they do for investigative work, often adding a 50 percent premium.

I have never seen the justification for this differential. A good expert works as hard and as carefully while investigating as when testifying. My own preference is to charge one rate satisfactory to me for all of my services whatever the circumstances. My preference is also to charge on an hourly basis, not to exceed an eight-hour charge in any one day.

Charges are on a portal-to-portal basis. Once you leave your office or home you are effectively working for your client, and you are unable to do other productive work. As a corollary, use travel time in the clients behalf to review documents or plan your investigation or presentation.

Any incidental, job-related, or travel expense should be billed in addition to the time charges, usually on a monthly basis. If considerable travel expense is involved, it may be desirable for a new client to provide transportation and lodging until you have developed a good working relationship. Similarly, if you find it necessary to purchase a significant dollar volume of subcontract services or supplies, you should arrange for the bills to be paid directly by the client attorney.

Who Pays

You will usually be paid for your services by the attorney who retains you either as a consultant or as a testifying expert. On occasion a plaintiff's attorney will indicate that you will be paid by the plaintiff. Unless the plaintiff has adequate resources and is known to you to have a good reputation for paying debts, this is probably an unsatisfactory arrangement.

The agreement to perform and be paid for services should be in the form of an agreement letter initiated by either the expert or the attorney. Copies should be signed by both parties setting out the terms and conditions. Suitable sample letters are shown in Appendix C. Once you have established a mutually satisfactory working relationship with a law firm you may elect to waive these formalities. But in the beginning make sure you have a clear written understanding.

You will be paid for your deposition time by the opposing attorney who is deposing you. You are also normally entitled to be paid for travel time by opposing counsel, although time spent in preparing for deposition is chargeable to your own client. On occasion the lawyers will agree that opposing counsel is liable only for the actual deposition time, all other expense to be borne by the client attorney. Make sure at deposition that you find out where to send your bill, and how the charges are to be divided between the lawyers.

When Are You Paid

When dealing with defense counsel representing a well-financed client, it is acceptable practice to bill on a monthly basis as you would any commercial client. You may have to wait some time for your payment. Your client will pay you when reimbursed by the defendant, usually an insurance company or self-insurer. Insurance companies are notorious for slow payment, but they will eventually pay all that you are owed.

There is a substantial difference in dealing with plaintiff's counsel, at least until you are satisfied with their financial stability and integrity. Plaintiff's counsel, usually paying the cost of the suit from their own pockets, are often reluctant to part with funds for expenses that did not result in a good settlement or a victory at trial. In the case of a plaintiff's counsel new to you, insist on a retainer to be paid in advance.

I once agreed to testify in a case in a technical area in which I had demonstrated expertise recognized by the local legal community. I didn't ask for a retainer to review the case before agreeing to consult with the attorney. I subsequently learned that the case was settled, that my potential involvement as an expert played some part in the settlement, and that the fee for my participation was zero. Since then I have changed my procedures.

I now request a retainer equal to one day's fee together with the full case file from any new potential plaintiff's counsel. For this amount I agree to review the file and report either orally or in writing my evaluation of their position from the technical viewpoint. More often than not this has proved acceptable. Where this has been a stumbling block, I was probably better off without the client. Again, this procedure is waived for clients with established relationships.

Once you agree to take a case, monthly billing together with a continuing need for your services is enough to insure payment on a timely basis. Some experts insist on advance progress payments throughout the case. I have never found this necessary, and only once in over thirty five years of intermittent forensic practice have I had a problem collecting a bill.

Witness Liability

The growth of the "let's sue" syndrome has apparently not left the expert witness immune. Although I am personally unaware of any case in which a technical expert has been sued for liability as a result of forensic activity, Feder[10] states that "troublesome is the witness's liability for negligence, which is a growing and fertile area for new claims against expert witnesses."

There is also an indication of a potential problem in the fact that NAFE (The National Academy of Forensic Engineers) offers professional liability insurance coverage to its members. The cost of this coverage is quite low, indicating that, at least so far, there have been very few unfortunate experiences.

My own belief is that the competent expert in forensic work has more protection from liability for negligence than does the engineer or scientist in the normal course of more routine professional activities. I have seen no need to protect my own forensic practice with liability coverage, and I have elected not to do so. This is, however, a personal business decision and not a general recommendation.

Entering forensic practice, you might want to consider special liability coverage. Or you may find that this activity is covered by professional "errors and omissions" insurance if you carry that. In any event it is something to think about.

CONTROLLING GROWTH

A primary difficulty in forensic practice is controlling growth. While this might ordinarily be considered a "high class" problem, there are some disturbing properties of forensics as part of a scientific or engineering business.

The first of these is the requirement that the personnel with the most technical experience in an organization must be actively involved in each project. In most scientific and engineering organizations this means top technical management. While line personnel can do much of the routine preparation, the critical activity of testifying at deposition and trial cannot be delegated.

The second problem is that of timing. Scheduling can be reasonably controlled until the time of trial. You are then at the mercy of the courts. Trials are scheduled, continued at the request of either counsel, rescheduled for the convenience of the court, and finally started at some indeterminate date. You must continually readjust your schedule to meet the changing agenda of the courts.

Once the case has started, the client attorney can give you some idea of when you will be called. If you are employed by plaintiff's attorney, the timing estimate may be reasonably close since plaintiff's case is presented first. The estimates of defense attorneys will be less accurate, because they have to guess at the time the plaintiff will take to present a case.

The estimates of both attorneys are subject to error depending on the priorities of the judge. I have known judges to keep court in session evenings and over weekends, thus moving the schedule ahead of the estimates. I have also been involved in cases where my testimony was delayed a week or more from the scheduled time when the judge held abbreviated sessions for reasons unknown to me.

Murphy's law applies. You will find that your testimony will almost always be scheduled when you would prefer, from a business standpoint, to be doing something else. Forensic activity feeds on its own success. You may find that the demands for your services at inconvenient times may exceed what you can supply without adversely affecting your other responsibilities.

This means either rejecting assignments, or hiring additional personnel. The decision is both subjective and objective. It should be made on the basis both of what you want to do with your time, and what you consider in the best interests of your business.

Finally, it is difficult to maintain an even mixture of plaintiff and defendant clients. As in the case of the law firms, it takes a deliberate effort to maintain this balance. Depending on the nature of your successes, one side or the other will seek you out energetically. If you wish to maintain any vestige of equality, a hard sales effort must be directed in the direction of imbalance.

Sooner or later you will be forced to choose assignments carefully, and to reject some work in the interests of maintaining impartiality. Nevertheless, either plaintiff's attorneys or defense attorneys will tend to dominate your client list.

If your organization is large you will probably be better off pointing your practice toward the defense. Most insurers analyze their exposure in any given case. If the exposure is high, the funds they allocate to defense are sufficient to warrant a major effort by a large technical organization.

If your organization is small, or if you are an individual practitioner, you may find it more interesting to work for a plaintiff-dominated clientele. In any case you should try to maintain some sort of balance. The client community will help you out on occasion. If you are particularly effective in certain types of cases, some law firms may try to retain you as a consultant to preempt your being hired by the opposition.

In the final analysis business judgments in forensic practice are similar to those in any service business. Choose your cases well. When rejecting cases, use the opportunity to upgrade the complexity and rewards of assignments that you accept. Maintain your honesty and integrity. Do the best job that you can at every opportunity and for every client. Follow these precepts and your forensic practice will grow to the limits of your ability to provide good service.

CHAPTER 15

Some Closing Thoughts

"And to make an end is to make a beginning. The end is where we start from."

—T. S. Eliot,
Little Gidding

PERSONAL REFLECTIONS

After many years and many experiences as an expert witness, there are still some things I wonder about from time to time. Here are a few questions that arise almost every time I become involved in someone else's dispute. Perhaps they offer some insights into the pros and cons of "expert witnessing" that this book has so far failed to convey.

How Do You Play When They Change the Rules?

The precise interpretation of the rules of expert testimony appear to vary with the jurisdiction, the inclinations of the judges, and the expectations of the lawyers. Meanwhile the U.S. Congress and the state legislatures strive continuously to make major structural changes in the basic foundation.

I have been involved in cases where technical excellence or, alternately, technical inadequacy was obvious. They were cases in which I could develop a strong technical argument to support my opinion. It was always frustrating to be told by a client attorney that I was probably right, but that the jurisdiction would render useless that testimony because of legal restrictions.

My only sometimes helpful solution has been to discuss with the client the jurisdictional rules and the interpretation of them after an initial reading of a case file, but before beginning a detailed investigation. If the rules effectively ban what the testimony will probably be, this is the place to stop. Otherwise you end up fighting a losing battle with your best hand tied behind your back.

Shall I Take This Case?

In my early years of practice I took some cases because I worked for companies that were in the business of accepting business. Too often I found myself on the wrong side of a dispute. These "losers" usually ended with a report concluding "It is suggested that you do not use this technical approach in pursuing your defense (or complaint)."

Today I accept cases where the nature of the incident appeals to my curiosity, where I think there is a technical challenge, where I have a positive first impression of both counsel and case, and where the economics are such as to justify the time necessary to do a substantive investigation. If any of these criteria are not met, I prefer to do other things.

What Makes A Good Expert Witness?

MacHovec[25] says "The best expert witnesses are stout-hearted, thick-skinned, and quick-witted." With the possible exception of "quick-witted" I am none of these things. Yet, based on the reaction of both clients and juries, I have experienced a fair degree of success in this field.

You really don't need the inborn qualities of a stout heart or thick skin until you are in court on the witness stand. And even then, some easily learned substitutes for these qualities can be very effective.

Never take a technical position with which you are not completely comfortable. Investigate meticulously. Prepare thoroughly. Know what message you want to communicate, and how best to do it. Never compromise your ethics or your honesty. Believe the things you intend to say. Do all of these things, and if you are a good expert, you will be a good expert witness.

What Am I Doing Here?

That question has flashed through my mind every time I've been on a witness stand. My feelings were expressed by Dickens in *Pickwick Papers* better than I can do it. "Battledore and shuttlecock's a very good game when you ain't the shuttlecock and two lawyers the battledores, in which case it gets too excitin' to be pleasant."

I've never learned to enjoy testifying in court, and I am always pleased when a case settles before that. On the other hand there is no career, to my knowledge, that does not have some unappealing facets. I testify because that is part of the job of being an expert witness. The fascinating aspects of the other activities associated with being a forensic expert make the occasional court appearances worthwhile to me.

Finally, I testify because I believe it's important. The courts need experts to help them make proper decisions about complex technical problems. I further believe the expert role to be essential to the fairness of both the entire civil dispute litigation process, and to the knowledgeable resolution of a dispute by a jury when that becomes necessary.

Am I Really Unbiased?

Sometimes in court under either direct or cross-examination I would find myself becoming emotionally involved in trying to express my thoughts. At times like that I wondered if I had remained the impartial expert I tried to be throughout all the preliminary proceedings, or if I had become an advocate for one side or the other.

Later I would realize that I was bringing to court only those opinions that I was certain were correct after months or sometimes years of thinking and rethinking. I had agonized over them until I had no doubt that my answers represented the best solutions to technical problems that had a number of possible solutions.

My emotional involvement was not with the client's cause, but with the importance of making the court understand and believe those opinions which were the result of my best professional efforts. If the opinions were developed honestly and fairly, a little positive emotion in conveying them was not bias but merely an aid to effective communication.

I could believe the absolute truth of my own technical testimony. I could argue effectively against contradictory technical evidence or experts, as in any scientific forum. And I could still be an unbiased expert witness for the purposes of civil litigation.

IN CONCLUSION

If you started this book from the beginning and are still reading, you have the interest and the knowledge to be a good expert witness. All you need in addition is some "hands on" experience with real cases. If you have had that experience, some of the thoughts that have been expressed here may help you improve your practice. If you haven't been through that exercise but are contemplating it, there is one last thing to consider.

Scientists and engineers for the most part are used to a cooperative rather than a combative forum for presenting and discussing their ideas. I have known some well-qualified specialists who handled a single case, who performed well up to and including trial, and who then took the position "never again." I have known others who were anxious for a second chance after an initial weak performance.

For the most part technical specialists who start forensic practice continue it because the advantages outweigh the drawbacks. Almost everyone experiences some trepidation at the prospect of defending a position in court against a trained lawyer. This fear is probably the main reason that technical specialists, otherwise qualified, avoid forensic practice.

There are great opportunities for service and reward for those who elect to build a practice in the forensic area. If you are considering it, but are still apprehensive about defending yourself against opposing lawyers, you may find some reassurance in the words from the "Letters" of Edna St. Vincent Millay. "I'm not so afraid of lawyers as I used to be. They are lambs in wolves clothing."

APPENDIX A

Bibliography and Source Directory

REFERENCES

1. ASTM: *ASTM Directory of Testing Laboratories*, ASTM, Philadelphia PA, 1991.
2. Best, A. M. Company: *Best's Insurance Reports-Property-Casualty*, A. M. Best Company, Oldwick NJ, 1990.
3. Black, H. C.: *Black's Law Dictionary*, West Publishing Company, St. Paul MN, 1991.
4. Blue, L.: *Jury Selection—Strategy and Science*, Callaghan, Wilmette IL, 1986.
5. Brown, P. M.: *The Art of Questioning*, Macmillan Publishing Co., New York NY, 1987.
6. Buchanan, J. C. and C. D. Bos: *How to Use Video in Litigation*, Prentice-Hall, Inc., Englewood Cliffs NJ, 1986.
7. Cacace, M. J.: Pres. Stamford CT Regional Bar Ass'n., "Why We Loathe Lawyers," *Orlando Sentinel*, Orlando FL, May 5, 1991.
8. Doyle, A. C.: *The Complete Sherlock Holmes, The Sign of Four*, Doubleday, Garden City NY, 1960.
9. Erlich, J. W.: *The Lost Art of Cross-Examination*, Dorset Press, New York NY, 1970.
10. Feder, H. A.: *Succeeding As An Expert Witness*, Van Nostrand Reinhold, New York NY, 1991.
11. Federal Rules of Evidence: 28 U.S.C.A. 2072–2074
12. Ferry, T. S.: *Modern Accident Investigation and Analysis*, John Wiley & Sons, New York NY, 1988.
13. Filter, D.: *The Demonstrative Evidence Sourcebook*, Stafford Hart Publications, Denver CO, 1985.

14. *Frye v. United States*: 293 Fed. 1013, DC Cir., 1923.
15. FTI: *FTI Demo Tape Version 4.2*, Forensic Technologies Int'l. Corp., Annapolis MD, 1988.
16. Hamlin, S.: *What Makes Juries Listen*, Law & Business, Inc., Clifton NJ, 1985.
17. Hendrick, K. and L. Benner, Jr.: *Investigating Accidents With STEP*, M. Dekker, New York NY, 1987.
18. Huff, D.: *How to Lie With Statistics*, W. W. Norton & Co. Inc., New York NY, 1954.
19. Johnson, W. G.: *MORT Safety Assurance Systems*, M. Dekker, New York NY, 1980.
20. Johnson, W. G.: *Accident/Incident Investigation Manual*, U.S. GPO, Washington DC, 1976.
21. Joiner, C. W.: *Civil Justice and the Jury*, Greenwood Press, Westport CT, 1962.
22. Kionka, E. J.: *Torts*, West Publishing Company, St Paul MN, 1988.
23. Kolb, J. and S. S. Ross: *Product Safety and Reliability*, McGraw-Hill Book Company, New York NY, 1980.
24. Leroux, G.: *J. Rouletabille, The Mystery of the Yellow Room*, Brentano's, New York, NY, 1908.
25. MacHovec, F. J.: *The Expert Witness Survival Manual*, C. C. Thomas, Springfield IL, 1987.
26. Mulligan, W. G.: *Expert Witnesses: Direct and Cross-Examination*, John Wiley and Sons, New York NY, 1987.
27. National Forensic Center: *The Guide to Experts' Fees*, National Forensic Center, Lawrenceville NJ, 1992.
28. Neely, R.: *The Product Liability Mess*, The Free Press, Division of Macmillan, Inc, New York NY, 1988.
29. Newton, Sir Issac: "Letter to Robert Hooke," 1675.
30. Olson, W. K.: *The Litigation Explosion*, Truman Talley Books-Dutton, Division Penguin Books, Inc., New York NY, 1991.
31. Paul, E.: *Homer Evans, Murder on the Left Bank*, Random House, New York NY, 1951.
32. SAE International: *Accident Reconstruction, State of the Art*, Society of Automotive Engineers, Warrendale PA, 1988.
33. SAE International: *Motor Vehicle Accident Reconstruction—Review and Update*, Society of Automotive Engineers, Warrendale PA, 1989.
34. Sullivan, C. D.: "Expert Witnesses—Or Are They?" *Defense Coun-*

sel Journal Vol. 58, No. 2, P.280, Int'l. Assn. of Defense Counsel, Chicago IL, April 1991.
35. Supreme Court: *Bates v. State Bar of Arizona*, 97 S. Ct. 2691 (1977).
36. *Supreme Court Reporter*: 111 S. Ct. 1032 (1991), West Publishing Company, St. Paul MN.
37. *Thomas Register of American Manufacturers:* and *Thomas Register Catalog File*, Thomas Publishing Co., New York NY, Annual.
38. U.S. Bureau of Alcohol, Tobacco, and Firearms: "ATF Arson Investigative Guide", U.S. GPO, Washington DC, 1985.
39. Weinstein, A. S. et al.: *Products Liability and the Reasonably Safe Product*, John Wiley & Sons, New York NY, 1978.
40. Wellman, F. L.: *The Art of Cross-Examination*, Dorset Press, New York NY, 1986.
41. Wenke, R. A.: *The Art of Selecting a Jury*, C. C. Thomas, Springfield IL, 1989.
42. Williams, A. L.: *All You Can Do Is All You Can Do, But All You Can Do Is Enough*, Oliver-Nelson, Nashville TN, 1988.
43. Witherell, C. E.: *How To Avoid Products Liability Lawsuits and Damages*, Noyes Publications, Park Ridge NJ, 1985.

SUPPLEMENTAL REFERENCES

The texts and documents listed below may be useful to the scientist or engineer interested in other aspects, more details, or different views of the skills needed to be a good expert witness. While not specifically referenced, their contents have been considered in writing this book.

Books

Alger, P. L. et al.: *Ethical Problems in Engineering*, John Wiley & Sons, New York NY, 1966.
A.S.T.M.: *Standards on Technical Aspects of Products Liability Litigation*, A.S.T.M., Philadelphia PA, 1988.
Blinn, K. W.: *Legal and Ethical Concepts in Engineering*, Prentice-Hall Publishing Co., Englewood Cliffs NJ, 1989.

Carper, K. L.: *Forensic Engineering*, Elsevier Science Publishing Co.,
   Inc., New York NY, 1989.
Dorram, P.: *The Expert Witness*, Planner's Press, Chicago IL, 1982.
Frankena, F. *The Scientist/Technician as Expert Witness*: A bibliography
   published by Vance Bibliographies, Monticello IL, 1985.
Lawrence, H. L.: *Settled Out of Court*, Aldine Publishing Co., Chicago
   IL, 1970.
Limpert, R.: *Motor Vehicle Accident Reconstruction and Cause Analy-
   sis*, The Michie Company, Charlottesville VA, 1989.
Perrow, C.: *Normal Accidents, Living with High-Risk Technolgies*,
   Basic Books, New York NY, 1984.
Phillips, J. J.: *Products Liability in a Nutshell*, West Publishing Co., St.
   Paul MN, 1988.
Poynter, D.: *The Expert Witness Handbook*, Para Publishing, Santa Bar-
   bara CA, 1987.
Thorpe, J. F.: *What Every Engineer Should Know About Product Lia-
   bility*, M. Dekker, New York NY, 1979.
Williams, C. A. and R. M. Heins: *Risk Management and Insurance*,
   McGraw-Hill Book Co., New York NY, 1989.
Wishman, S.: *Anatomy of a Jury*, Penguin Books, New York NY, 1986.

Periodicals

Experts should maintain state-of-the-art proficiency through review
of technical periodicals in their own field of specialization. The following nontechnical periodicals are useful for providing information about
the legal aspects of expert witness services, offering leads for business
expansion, and serving as advertising media.

ABA Journal: Magazine published monthly by the American Bar Association, Chicago IL. Distributed primarily to all members of the ABA.
   Good advertising medium.
Claims: Magazine published monthly by IW Publications, Seattle WA,
   serving the insurance claims industry. Originally published as *Insurance Adjuster*. Good advertising medium.
For The Defense: Magazine published monthly by the Defense Research

Institute, Inc., Chicago IL. Defense, insurance, and corporate counsel orientation.

The National Law Journal: Newspaper published weekly by the New York Law Publishing Co., New York NY. Good advertising medium.

Trial: Magazine published monthly by the Association of Trial Lawyers of America, Washington DC. Plaintiff's counsel orientation. Good advertising medium.

Additionally most state and local bar associations publish monthly magazines and newspapers which may serve as good advertising media. Check your local library for availability.

Legal Support Activities

The following resources provide information useful in the preparation of cases for litigation. Intended primarily for attorneys, they also provide the technical expert with potential sources for subcontract services. They are all good sources for business expansion, some as advertising media, others as direct sources of work on a fixed fee or fee-sharing basis.

Directory of Forensic Specialists: Published annually as part of the June edition of Claims magazine, IW Publications, Seattle WA.

Encyclopedia of Legal Information Sources: A bibliographic guide to about 19,000 sources of information on over 450 legal subjects including expert witness technique. Gale Research Co., Detroit MI, 1988.

Forensic Services Directory: Listing fee. Hard copy as well as national computerized data bases. Published annually by the National Forensic Center, Lawrenceville NJ.

Lawyers Desk Reference: Published by Lawyers Co-operative Pub. Co., Rochester NY., 1987 (annual updates).

Technical Advisory Service for Attorneys (TASA): National expert witness referral service. Acts as business manager, adding burden to normal witness fee in quoting prices. Supplies experts to attorneys in about 4500 categories from computerized data base. Blue Bell PA.

Forensic and Technical Support Organizations

There are numerous reputable organizations nationwide providing technical forensic investigation services, technical support services, and expert consultant and witness services as needed. The following list represents a brief sampling of the types of organizations that exist. Examination of the classified telephone directory of any major city will yield many others.

All of these organizations, in addition to their staff personnel, employ outside consultants in various specialties to expand corporate capability.

Forensic Technologies International Corporation—Annapolis MD. Professional employee and consulting staff of one hundred plus personnel. In-house laboratories, library, exhibit preparation facilities, computer generated video simulation. Trains and prepares personnel for deposition and trial by use of company attorneys assuming role of opposition counsel.

Garrett Forensic Engineers—Los Angeles CA. Professional employee and consulting staff of two hundred plus personnel. Branches in Nevada, Arizona, Colorado and Texas. Broad spectrum of skills. In-house video and graphic capabilities.

Impact General, Inc.—Orange CA. Professional employee and consulting staff of 300 plus personnel. National Institute of Forensic Studies division provides instruction for claims people and attorneys. In-house metallurgical, chemical, and soils laboratories.

Inter-City Testing & Consulting Corporation—Mineola NY. Provides technical (as well as medical and dental) services to the legal profession, insurance companies, industry and government. Offers a full range of forensic services in all major fields of science and engineering.

Triodyne Inc.—Niles IL. Affiliates include Institute for advanced safety studies. In-house test laboratories, machine shops, graphic communications capability, on-line library. Publishes "Safety Brief," limited distribution newsletter containing useful information for both attorneys and technical specialists. Company provides safety studies and full litigation support services.

APPENDIX B

Glossary

Accident reconstruction—Establishing the most probable scenario for an accident by scientific review of physical, testimonial, and documentary evidence.

Adversary system—The laws and procedures by which parties to a dispute argue against each other before a "trier of fact" who decides which argument prevails.

Affidavit—A written statement of fact made voluntarily under oath before a person authorized to administer such an oath, e.g., a notary public.

Affirmative defense—A defense that admits the facts of a complaint, but denies the legal right of the plaintiff to sue because of contributory negligence, assumption of risk, statute of limitations, or other legal precepts.

Allegation—An assertion by a party to a suit during pleading that states the nature of the issues to be proved in court.

Amicus curiae—(Lat.: friend of the court), a person not a party to a suit who petitions the court to present information on behalf of one of the parties to the suit, or because of personal interest in the outcome.

Answer—A defendant's first pleading; a written multi-page response to a complaint usually summarized as "it didn't happen, but if it did I didn't do it, but if I did it was someone else's fault, maybe yours."

Assumption of risk—An affirmative defense that the plaintiff was aware of an obviously dangerous situation, yet accepted the exposure voluntarily.

Beyond a reasonable doubt—The standard of proof in criminal trials. Requires a high (but not absolute) degree of certainty in the mind of an ordinary person.

Burden of proof—The need for a party making an allegation to offer proof in court of its validity within the probabilities required by the controlling law: i.e., beyond a reasonable doubt, clear and convincing evidence, preponderance of the evidence.

Case law—The interpretations by the courts of the meaning of the law in similar cases, as opposed to the laws themselves.

Causation—The act which causes something to happen, usually essential in proving negligence.

Chain of custody—An accounting of the control of physical evidence up to the time it is presented in court to assure that it has not been significantly altered.

Claim—An assertion and demand that one is entitled to money or property, often leading to a suit if the demand is not met.

Clear and convincing evidence—A standard of proof in some civil cases which falls somewhere between "beyond a reasonable doubt" and "a preponderance of the evidence."

Comparative negligence—A determination of the relative percentages of fault of the plaintiff and defendant. Awards are reduced by the percentage of plaintiff negligence.

Complaint—The first pleading of a plaintiff, a multi-page document which can be summarized as saying "I suffered an injury because you didn't do all of these things you should have done, and you did all these things you shouldn't have done."

Conflict of interest—A situation where prior knowledge, prior commitment, or the prospect of personal gain casts doubt on the impartiality of professional services.

Conjecture—An opinion which explains the facts, but which is not based on evidence strong enough to support the opinion.

Contingency fee—Payment for services based on the outcome of a suit, usually as a percentage of the award.

Contributory negligence—A claim that plaintiff failed to observe reasonable, prudent, and obvious safety precautions. If a defendant can prove contributory negligence, the plaintiff is usually precluded from receiving any damage award.

Counterclaim—A demand by the defendant against the plaintiff as an independent action, and not necessarily a direct response to the plaintiff's claim.

Court reporter—An officer of the court who transcribes court proceedings, not always with unerring accuracy. On occasion witnesses may have difficulty interpreting their own testimony from transcripts.

Cross-claim—A claim by a defendant against another defendant, or a plaintiff against another plaintiff rather than against the opposition.

Cross-examination—Questioning by opposing counsel with the intent of weakening the testimony, or impairing the credibility of a witness who has provided damaging testimony on direct examination at a trial or deposition.

Cross interrogatory—An interrogatory by a person who has been interrogated served on any other parties to the suit.

Curriculum vitae—(Lat.: the course of one's life), a brief resume of educational and professional qualifications.

Damages—Monetary compensation awarded by a court to one who has proved injury by another.

Deep pockets—A defendant having adequate resources to assure that an anticipated judgment can be paid.

Defect—A deficiency which makes a product unsafe for use, e.g., manufacturing defect, design defect, failure to warn, failure to maintain, etc.

Defendant—The one who is sued to recompense the one suing for alleged injury.

Demeanor evidence—The behavior of the witness on the stand, including appearance, bearing, apparent truthfulness, confidence, and facial expression are permissible issues for the trier of fact to consider in determining credibility.

Demonstrative evidence—Aids (photographs, charts, videotapes, models, computer graphics, etc.) which are used to clarify the testimony of a witness. Without accompanying testimony, demonstrative evidence is not probative.

Demurrer—An allegation by a defendant that even if the facts stated in a complaint are true, they are insufficient for the case to proceed.

Deponent—One who gives information under oath, usually at deposition.

Deposition—Part of the pretrial discovery process where a witness testifies under oath with the proceedings transcribed by a court reporter. The opposing attorney asks the questions to assess your position. Friendly counsel may cross-examine.

Destructive testing—Test methods which destroy or permanently alter the nature of the evidence, e.g., structural testing of a support assembly to failure. Should not be done without the concurrence and observation of the opposition.

Direct examination—The first questioning of a witness by the attorney who has called the witness to support a case.

Discovery—The pretrial process of finding out what the other side thinks and intends to do, based on interrogatories, depositions, investigation, production, and documentation.

Expert testimony—Presentation and explanation by a person having special skill or training not possessed by the average person, about phenomena in the area of expertise which help the "trier of fact" understand the issues more clearly. This testimony may include professional opinions.

Expert witness—A person who, by reason of training and experience, has specialized knowledge in a field not easily understood by persons without such background, and where such understanding is necessary to reach proper conclusions.

Forensics—The application of scientific or engineering technology in support of legal proceedings.

Frye rule—Case law which holds that expert testimony must be based on scientific principles generally accepted by the professional community of which the expert is a part.

Gross negligence—Intentional failure to carry out a clear duty with reckless disregard of the consequences of injury to another.

Hypothetical question—A question framed to elicit expert opinion from a witness based on assumptions claimed to be facts in evidence. The witness is told to assume the facts are true, and then is asked to form an opinion, if possible, based on those facts.

Impeachment of witness—An attack on the credibility of a witness by showing inconsistency, bias, or character defect.

Inadmissible evidence—Evidence which, while true and significant, cannot be used because of constraints of the law.

Injury—wrong or damage to person, property, rights, or reputation.

Insurance—An agreement by one party to reimburse another for certain losses under certain conditions, usually in return for money paid as premiums. Use of the word "insurance" should be avoided in court because it can form the basis for a mistrial.

Interrogatories—Written questions served on an adversary who must respond in writing under oath. Used early in the discovery process, typically before deposition of technical experts.

Judgment—An official decision by a court concerning a matter brought before it.

Jurisdiction—The areas of authority of a court with regard to geography, subject matter, parties involved, and the powers of the court.

Last clear chance—A defense in some jurisdictions against the allegation of contributory negligence. If defendant had an opportunity to avoid injuring the plaintiff after the plaintiff's contributory negligence ceased, some courts will allow an award to the plaintiff.

Latent defect—A defect that is not obvious to the reasonably careful observer, e.g., a casting flawed by internal cracking.

Leading question—A question posed by a lawyer that suggests the desired answer. Usually improper on direct examination, they are often allowed on cross-examination or when questioning a hostile witness.

Liability—An obligation to do something or to refrain from doing something. Responsibility for the consequences of one's conduct.

Material evidence—Evidence which has a direct bearing on the issue in dispute, and which tends to influence the "trier of fact" because of its rational connection to the case.

Motion—Written or oral requests to the court by attorneys before, during, or after trial. Motions are made with reference to particular actions which are within judicial discretion.

Motion for summary judgment—A motion asking for favorable judgment by the court without trial where only questions of law, and not questions of fact, are in dispute.

Motion in limine—A motion to prohibit the introduction of irrelevant, inadmissible, or highly prejudicial material. If granted, may prevent the use of some demonstrative evidence.

Negligence—Failure to do what a reasonable and prudent person would do under given circumstances, or doing what a reasonable and prudent person would not do.

Nondestructive testing—Testing which leaves the test item unaltered, e.g., X ray, linear measurement, micrography, etc.

Objection—The act by an attorney of calling the attention of the court to an improper question, statement, or the introduction of improper evidence by the opposition.

Patent defect—A defect that is obvious to the reasonably careful observer, e.g., exposed and charred electrical wiring.

Perjury—The criminal offense of lying under oath.

Plaintiff—The party who starts suit in a civil action.

Pleadings—The formal written statements presented sequentially by opposing sides in a suit. They outline the plaintiff's cause for action, and the defendant's grounds for defense. Their purpose is to define precisely the issues to be tried.

Preponderance of evidence—A weight of evidence indicating a "more likely than not" truth. The usual standard of proof in civil cases. More than 50 percent probability is enough in the eyes of the law, but often not in the minds of a jury.

Prima facie case—(Lat.: At first view), A case in which the evidence supports but does not compel a favorable decision. A case that will usually win in the absence of strong contradictory evidence.

Privilege—A benefit accruing to certain classes of persons not available to others, e.g., communication between lawyer and client, or a lawyer's work product are ordinarily privileged and cannot be discovered by the opposition.

Probative—Having the effect of proof, tending to prove the truth of facts or allegations.

Proximate cause—That cause which sets in motion a chain of events resulting in an accident without the intervention of any other cause, and without which the accident would not have happened. The last negligent act contributing to an injury.

Reasonable and prudent person—A hypothetical person who exercises the standards of intelligence and judgment necessary for the safety of society. The necessary extent of these qualities is usually a matter for jury decision.

Rebuttal—The introduction of evidence by an attorney to counteract evidence or facts introduced by the opposition after the attorney has rested the case.

Redirect examination—Questioning of the witness by the original examiner after cross-examination to clarify or weaken points made during cross-examination.

Request for admission—A written statement of facts concerning a case which are submitted to the opposition for admission or denial. Only those facts denied will be the subject of trial.

Request for production—A written request to produce documents for inspection and copying, or hardware for inspection and testing.

Res ipsa loquitur—(Lat.: The thing speaks for itself), a case in which the inference of negligence may be made on the basis that an accident could not have happened without it. The effect is to shift the burden of proof from the plaintiff to the defendant.

Rest the case—Said by an attorney who has completed presentation of all evidence.

Retainer—A fee paid to an attorney or expert witness by a client when retained to act on behalf of the client.

Scientific certainty—Proved beyond a reasonable doubt by means of technical analysis or testing.

Scientific probability—Proved as more probable than not by means of technical analysis or testing.

Sequester—(Witnesses), exclude witnesses from court until it is time for their testimony, usually to avoid influencing that testimony by the prior testimony of other witnesses.

Side-bar—Position at the judge's bench where counsel meet with judge (and usually court reporter) during trial to discuss matters inappropriate for the jury to hear.

Speculation—Theorizing that is not supported by sufficient evidence to meet the required level of probability.

Statute of limitations—The time after an incident during which legal action must be started to allow recovery of damages, usually varying among jurisdictions.

Stipulation—Agreement between opposing attorneys as to the truth of certain facts, the admissibility of evidence, the qualification of expert witnesses, or other items incidental to legal proceedings.

Strict liability—Liability without the need to show fault, applicable when a product is sold in a defective condition unreasonably dangerous to the user. May be applied even where the seller has taken all reasonable precautions in making and selling the product.

Subpoena—A legal command for a witness to appear at a certain time and place to give testimony about a matter in litigation.

Subpoena duces tecum—A subpoena requiring the witness to bring documents, books, notes, photographs, specifications, raw data, test results, etc. to the place of appearance.

Subrogate—Assign the rights in a legal procedure to another, e.g., an insurance company, having paid a claim, may be assigned the right to sue any entity that the party compensated could have sued rather than exercising an insurance claim.

Suit—Any legal proceeding in a court of law in which one party seeks any remedy the law provides for injury caused by another.

Testimony—Statements by a witness made orally under oath as distinguished from those made in writing.

Third party complaint—A complaint filed by a defendant in a suit against a third party not previously named in the suit. The allegation is usually that the third party is liable for some or all of the damages that might be awarded if the defendant loses.

Tort—Causing a civil injury through the neglect of a legal obligation to an injured party, where such neglect was the direct cause of the injury.

Transcript—The official record of a trial or other legal proceeding as transcribed by a court reporter.

Trier of fact—The jury in a jury trial, and the judge when a jury trial has been waived.

Verdict—The formal decision of the jury concerning the matters of fact assigned for its consideration and determination by the court.

Voir dire—Examination by attorneys or the court of prospective jurors to determine their qualification and fitness for jury duty in a specific case.

Work product—Notes, impressions, memoranda, legal research, and other materials used by an attorney in anticipation of legal proceedings. This information is usually protected from discovery by the opposition.

APPENDIX C

Technical Records and Reports

The following sample forms, letters, and reports are generic, and typical of what might be created during the course of preparing a case for trial. They are by no means exhaustive and should be altered to suit the needs of the individual practitioner and case. The client's legal strategy will determine the degree of documentation to some extent.

In many cases a client will request that no report at all be prepared. Under these circumstances keep notes sufficient to refresh your memory if a report is ultimately required, but avoid gratuitous observations.

In other cases a complete report of everything you have done and considered may be requested. These requests should be answered with a full-fledged report typical of what might be prepared in an industry or university development project.

Most often a requested report will be used in mediation, and should be limited to what was done and what was concluded on the basis of that work. The report samples included here meet that need. They are intended to supply the essential facts without disclosing lengthy details of the reasoning processes. If the opposition wants more information, make them ask for it.

Figure 2   Sample Contact Memorandum form.
Letter 1   Expert-originated agreement letter.
Letter 2   Client-originated agreement letter.
Figure 3   Sample Site Survey Agenda form.
Figure 4   Sample Site Survey Summary form.
Figure 5   Sample Evidence Custody form.
Report 1   Sample Plaintiff-oriented report.*
Report 2   Sample Defense-oriented report.*

*Note that whichever report format is used, the report must reflect true and unbiased opinions based on observed facts.

CONTACT MEMORANDUM

Date __2/30/99__   Time __2:15 PM__

Contact Name: John Jones, Esq. — Smith, Smith, Smith & Jones

Address: 1234 Main Street — Anytown, USA

                              Contact Type: Phone call

Telephone: (407) 555-1111

Representing: John Doe and spouse

Plaintiff or Defendant: Plaintiff

Versus: The XYZ Manufacturing Company et al.

       Complaint not filed — Defense counsel unknown

What Happened: John Doe was working his normal shift at the Anytown Steel Co. operating an XYZ1000 Robot which was feeding metal sheets to a rolling mill. The Robot suddenly turned, seized Mr. Doe, and forced his arm into the mill, resulting in serious injury.

When: Date 1/11/99 Time 1:15 AM

Where: Anytown Steel Co. — 4444 Industrial Avenue Anytown, USA

Consultant or Witness: Consultant   Accept or Decline: Accept

Remarks: Available Evidence—plant accident report, police report, ambulance and medical reports, OSHA report, witness statements, documentation provided by XYZ to Anytown Steel with Robot. Will visit site on date to be set after reviewing copies of Fed. Exp. documentation. ($1000 advance approved).

FIGURE 2

EXPERT LETTERHEAD

March 3, 1999

Smith, Smith, Smith & Jones, P.A.
1234 Main Street
Anytown, USA

      Attn: John Jones, Esq.
      Re: Doe vs XYZ Manufacturing Co.

Dear Mr. Jones:

Thank you for your interest in using my consulting services in the above referenced matter. Enclosed is my curriculum vitae in accordance with your request.

Confirming our telephone discussion, I would like to review all accident reports, witness statements, machinery documents (operator, maintenance, and parts manuals), photographs, and other pertinent material for preliminary evaluation.

After examining that material, I will make arrangements with you to visit the accident site, examine the machinery, and talk to any witnesses that are available.

My charge for this service is $xxx per hour, not to exceed $xxxx in any one working day. The total cost for this initial effort including travel expense and the preparation of a short report is estimated at $xxxx.

As we discussed, I require a retainer of $xxxx prior to starting any new project. This retainer will be credited at $xxx per hour.

If you have any further questions please do not hesitate to call.

Very truly yours,

James X. Pert

LETTER 1

CLIENT LETTERHEAD

March 3, 1999

James X. Pert, P.E.
3333 Research Drive
Technitown, USA

Re: Doe vs. XYZ Manufacturing Co.

Dear Mr. Pert:

The purpose of this letter is to confirm that we wish to retain your services in the investigation and prosecution of the above referenced case. Enclosed please find our check in the amount of $xxxx as a retainer in this matter to be credited at the rate of $xxx per hour.

Also enclosed for your review are the following materials.

1. Factory, police, paramedic, and OSHA accident reports.
2. Statements by John Doe (injured party), F. Johnson (Steel Co. manager), E. Edwards (maintenance mechanic), and D. Douglas (co-worker eyewitness).
3. Operator manual, maintenance manual, and parts list for the XYZ1000 industrial robot.
4. Photographs of site and machine by our investigator.

If there are any other items or documents you need for your evaluation of this case, please advise me and we will try to get them for you.

As soon as you have completed your preliminary examination, please call so that we can arrange for your visit to the accident site for examination of the machinery involved.

I look forward to working with you in this matter.

Sincerely,

John Jones

LETTER 2

SITE SURVEY AGENDA

Date 4/11/99

Contact Name: Frank Johnson — Plant Mgr. — Anytown Steel Co.
Location: 4444 Industrial Ave.—Anytown, USA
Phone: (407) 555-2222   Job Number:

Talk to: F. Johnson, E. Edwards (maintenance mechanic),
                D. Douglas (eyewitness).

Examine: XYZ Industrial Robot model XYZ1000 SN 9876,
                mill involved, site geometry, machine safeguards,
                XYZ installation drawings and instructions,
                service area, maintenance records, Anytown safety
                manual and training procedures.

Measure: site geometry, radio frequency background, time
                study of machinery by real time videotape, noise
                levels.

Instruments and Tools: mechanical & optical linear measurement
                equipment, noise level meter, RFI instruments,
                video and still cameras.

Support Services: Commercial Photo & Video (photos/videotapes)
                Radiation Group (RFI measurements).

Remarks: Get all information possible on first visit.
                May not get second visit authorization.

FIGURE 3

ACCIDENT SITE SURVEY SUMMARY

Date   4/11/99   Time   10:30 AM

Case:	Doe vs. XYZ et al.
Contact Name:	Frank Johnson—Plant Mgr.—Anytown Steel Co.
Address:	4444 Industrial Ave.—Anytown, USA
	Phone: (407) 555-2222

Persons Present: J. Jones, Wm. Williams (defense counsel),
                         F. Johnson, Edw. Edwards (mechanic), Bob Roberts
                         (defense expert), J. Joseph (plant safety rep.).
                         M. Milton (Commercial Photo and Video Corp.)

Arrival Time at Site: 11:05 AM   Departure Time: 15:45 PM

Case Discussed With: Jones, Johnson, Edwards, Joseph, Milton,
                         A. Andrews (equipment operator—casual talk)

Measurements: Site geometry. Time study of XYZ1000 Robot
                         S.N. 9876 with mill involved in accident. Time
                         study of similar equipment by ABC Robot Mfg. Co.
                         Noise levels. Cancel RFI—instrument problems.

Documents: Installation and operating instructions/drawings
                         by XYZ. Anytown Steel operating and safety docs.
                         Anytown Steel maintenance records for all Robots.

Remarks: Videotape and photography of accident scene and
                         equipment operation by Commercial Photo. Other
                         photos and Polaroid shots by myself. Requested
                         copy of Anytown Steel safety manual. Response
                         deferred. D. Douglas (eyewitness) unavailable—
                         changed employment. Radiation Group unavailable.

FIGURE 4

EVIDENCE CUSTODY RECORD

Date 5/8/99

Case: Doe vs. XYZ et al.

Attorney: John Jones, Esq.

Address: 1234 Main Street — Anytown, USA

                                    Phone: (407) 555-1111

Description: Broken widget received from Mr. Jones this date.
                  Item was in plastic bag and in condition shown in
                  attached Polaroid. Identifying initials (AES) were
                  marked on edge of each piece.

Handling Log: 5/8/99 Item received. Placed in locked storage.
                  5/17/99 Taken to lab for nondestructive testing.
                  (X ray, hardness, photos. Surveillance maintained.
                  5/17/99 Placed in locked storage.
                  5/22/99 Microscopic exam & return to storage.
                  5/23/99 Delivered to offices of defense counsel,
                  W. Williams, Esq.

Remarks: Both pieces of widget show small indentations in
                  undamaged area as a result of hardness testing.

Transfer Record: This item of evidence released as received
                  except as noted under "Remarks."

Received by: Date:

FIGURE 5

REPORT FORM HEADING—(Plaintiff)

August 10, 1999

Smith, Smith, Smith & Jones, P.A.
1234 Main Street
Anytown, USA

      Attn: John Jones Esq.
      Re: Doe vs. XYZ Manufacturing Co.

Pursuant to your request and authorization of March 3, 1999, I have reviewed the circumstances concerning the accident to John Doe at the Anytown Steel Company facility in Anytown, USA on or about January 11, 1999.

I have assessed background information supplied by you, as well as the following material.

1. Miscellaneous documents including accident reports, shipping documents, and warranty service reports.
2. Complaint dated June 2, 1999—Doe vs. XYZ Mfg. Co.
3. Notice for discovery and inspection, and response of defendant XYZ Manufacturing Co.
4. Deposition transcript of the plaintiff, John Doe.
5. Deposition transcript of Frank Johnson, Anytown Steel Company plant manager.
6. Deposition transcript of E. Edwards, Anytown Steel Co. maintenance mechanic.
7. Deposition transcript of J. Joseph, Anytown Steel Co. plant safety representative.
8. Owners and Operators Guide for XYZ1000 series Industrial Robot for machine SN 9876.
9. Service and parts manuals for XYZ1000 Robot SN 9876.
10. XYZ Company quality control procedures.

I have also reviewed the American National Safety Standard for Industrial Robots, ANSI xxx.x-199x. The 199x version of this safety standard was in effect at the time that this robot was manufactured.

Finally, I examined the accident site and involved machinery on April 31, 1999. At that time, I also discussed the accident informally with Johnson, Edwards, and Joseph. Any information provided by them is reaffirmed in their deposition testimony.

ACCIDENT SUMMARY

Mr. Doe was operating a model XYZ1000 Industrial Robot as a sheet feed mechanism for a Pitbull Model 4 rolling mill. During the normal course of operations, and without warning, the robot seized Mr. Doe by the wrist, forced his arm between the mill rolls, and thus injured his arm. The robot continued to hold Mr. Doe, and the mill continued to operate until power to the machinery was disconnected by Mr. D. Douglas (undeposed witness no longer employed by Anytown Steel Co.).

RESULTS OF INVESTIGATION

Examination of the Robot revealed that the widget (XYZ part number 12803B) connecting the left appendage to the drive motor had broken, permitting the appendage to assume any random position through a ninety degree arc at the start of a cycle. Under these conditions the "grip" mechanism and the "rotary" mechanism would continue to function normally, but the "grab" position would be altered in an uncontrolled manner.

Moreover, a significant deviation from Safety Standard ANSI xxx.x-199x was observed. This standard requires that all industrial robots be equipped with "a pull-cord operated switch fastened to an operator safety belt capable of disconnecting all power to the robot in an emergency." A switch of this type was not present on the XYZ1000 Robot at the time of the accident.

MOST PROBABLE SCENARIO

The XYZ Robot was manufactured with a cast aluminum widget which failed due either to inadequate design, or to a defect in the casting during fabrication. As a result of this failure the Robot was able to seize Mr. Doe's arm rather than the feed stock at the start of a feed cycle. The rest of the cycle was normal for the Robot, with the retained item being fed to the mill rolls. Mr. Doe's arm was thus fed to the mill rolls, and he was unable to avoid or minimize his injuries due to the absence of the kill-switch required by the standard.

CONCLUSION

It is my opinion that the proximate cause of this accident was the unreasonably dangerous design of the robot which allowed the broken widget to put it in a fail-dangerous rather than a fail-safe condition. The design should have caused the robot to stop upon widget failure, rather than allowing it to operate in an uncontrolled manner.

It is also my opinion that the widget was defective either in design or manufacture at the time the Robot SN 9876 left the factory.

Finally, It is my opinion that Mr. Doe acted in a reasonable and prudent manner for a robot operator. His inability to avoid or minimize the injury was a direct result of the absence of a pull type safety switch where he could reach it.

Very truly yours,

James X. Pert

REPORT FORM HEADING—(Defendant)

Note: The defense-oriented report can be similar to the plaintiff-oriented report through the accident summary. The information submitted to that point is a matter of fact. The reports will differ only in what documents, statements, and observations were made, and in some cases may not differ at all.

September 18, 1999

Williams and Williams, P.A.
1234 Main Street
Anytown, USA

       Attn: Wm. Williams, Esq.
       Re: Doe vs. XYZ Manufacturing Co.

Pursuant to your request and authorization of July 3, 1999, I have reviewed the circumstances concerning the accident to John Doe at the Anytown Steel Company facility in Anytown, USA on or about January 11, 1999.

I have assessed background information supplied by you, as well as the following material.

1. Miscellaneous documents including accident reports, shipping documents, and warranty service reports.
2. Complaint dated June 2, 1999—Doe vs. XYZ Mfg. Co.
3. Notice for discovery and inspection, and response of defendant XYZ Manufacturing Co.
4. Deposition transcript of the plaintiff, John Doe.
5. Deposition transcript of Frank Johnson, Anytown Steel Company plant manager.
6. Deposition transcript of E. Edwards, Anytown Steel Co. maintenance mechanic.
7. Deposition transcript of J. Joseph, Anytown Steel Co. plant safety representative.
8. Owners and Operators Guide for XYZ1000 series Industrial Robot for machine SN 9876.

9. Service and parts manuals for XYZ1000 Robot SN 9876.
10. XYZ Company quality control procedures.
11. Report of James X. Pert dated August 10, 1999.

I have also reviewed the American National Safety Standard for Industrial Robots, ANSI xxx.x-199x. The 199x version of this safety standard was in effect at the time that this robot was manufactured.

Finally, I examined the accident site and involved machinery on July 15, 1999. At that time, I also discussed the accident informally with Messrs. Johnson and Edwards. Any information provided by them is reaffirmed in their deposition testimony.

ACCIDENT SUMMARY

Mr. Doe was operating a model XYZ1000 Industrial Robot as a sheet feed mechanism for a Pitbull Model 4 rolling mill. During the normal course of operations, and without warning, the robot seized Mr. Doe by the wrist, forced his arm between the mill rolls, and thus injured his arm. The robot continued to hold Mr. Doe, and the mill continued to operate until power to the machinery was disconnected by Mr. D. Douglas (undeposed witness no longer employed by Anytown Steel Co.).

RESULTS OF INVESTIGATION

Examination of the Robot revealed that the widget (XYZ part number 128038) connecting the left appendage to the drive motor had broken, permitting the appendage to assume any random position through a ninety degree arc at the start of a cycle. Under these conditions the "grip" mechanism and the "rotary" mechanism would continue to function normally, but the "grab" position would be altered in an uncontrolled manner.

Moreover, a significant deviation from Safety Standard ANSI xxx.x-199x was observed. This standard requires that all industrial robots be equipped with "a pull-cord operated switch fastened to an operator safety belt capable of disconnecting all power to the robot in an emergency." A switch of this type was not present on the XYZ1000 Robot at the time of the accident.

XYZ Company indicates that this machine was shipped from the factory with the safety switch in place and operational. Mounting holes for this switch were present on the robot, and wear of the paint around the holes (Photo. 1) indicates the switch to have been present at one time.

Examination of the rolling mill revealed that a proper guard to prevent the operator from being harmed by the "pinch point" of the rollers was loose, and was not equipped with an electrical interlock to stop the mill under these conditions (Photo 2).

MOST PROBABLE SCENARIO

The failed widget shows signs of abuse, apparently during maintenance (Photo 3). As a result of this failure the Robot was able to malfunction, allegedly causing harm to Mr. Doe. Mr. Doe's arm was thus fed to the mill rolls, and seized by the rolls due to the absence of a proper guard. Moreover, Mr. Doe was unable to avoid or minimize his injuries due to the absence of the kill-switch required by the standard.

CONCLUSION

It is my opinion that the proximate cause of this accident was a lack of proper maintenance resulting in a broken widget, combined with the failure of the rolling mill to be equipped with a proper guard and electrical safety interlock.

It is also my opinion that the damage was exacerbated by the removal of the safety cord from the robot, apparently during maintenance procedures by the owner.

Finally, It is my opinion that Mr. Doe, as an experienced operator, should have recognized the clear danger of operating this machinery without a guard on the mill, and a safety lanyard on the robot. His negligence in ignoring prudent operating technique was a major factor in causing this accident.

Very truly yours,

Frank R. E. Buttal

APPENDIX D

Investigator's Tool Kit

Measurement, testing, sampling, and photo-recording are essential to almost every technical accident investigation. Ideally the investigator should have a mobile laboratory and shop available at the accident site during the site survey. In the real world this rarely happens. There are a number of physical restrictions on the assets that can be deployed effectively.

Consideration must be given in advance to site accessibility, opportunity to revisit the site if desired, probable cooperation of site personnel, and the availability of local technical support services on a priority basis if needed.

The basic equipment listed below should be a part of every investigator's "carry along" tool kit. The supplementary and special equipment may be supplied by the investigator if the mode of transportation to the site permits. Alternately, other arrangements to have this equipment available should be made in advance if its need is anticipated.

GENERAL PURPOSE BASIC EQUIPMENT

1. Measuring tape—Stanley 20-foot Powerlock or equal.
2. Multiple lens magnifier—Bausch and Lomb 5x–20x or equal.
3. Six inch rule—Starrett four edge or equal.
4. Small flashlight—Mini-Maglite or equal.
5. Caliper—Starrett 6-inch pocket slide caliper or equal.
6. Swiss army knife—maximum number of blades and tools.
7. Magnet—small (identification of magnetic materials).
8. Sample containers—appropriate for expected sample types.

9. Small screw and nut driver set.
10. Small needle-nose and side cutting pliers.
11. Microcassette recorder.
12. Pocket notebook.

SPECIAL PURPOSE BASIC EQUIPMENT

Each scientific discipline has its own set of small specialty field measurement and sampling items which are appropriate to most technical field investigations. To the extent that these can be carried without making the basic "carry along" kit overly burdensome, they should be included. The following list is intended to be representative rather than inclusive for both specialties and for equipment. Experts in each specialty should prepare their own lists.

Arson—Electronic accelerant detector.
Civil—Optical level, ultrasonic tape measure.
Electrical—Wire gage, AC-DC multimeter, clamp-on AC meter.
Chemical—pH tester, special sampling devices.
Environmental—Ringelmann chart, dust sample collectors.
Heating and Air Cond.—anemometer, psychrometer, thermometer.
Illumination—Reflected and incident light photometers.
Mechanical—Tachometer, thickness and screw pitch gages.
Metallurgical—Hardness tester, surface comparison blocks.
Structural—Dye check kit, safety lanyard, sound level meter.
Water Analysis—Quality test kit, BOD sampler.

TOOLS AND SUPPORT EQUIPMENT

A full assortment of general and special purpose tools and industrial equipment are required for a reasonably high percentage of field investigations. For example, the removal and disassembly for inspection of an industrial engine and transmission in the field requires not only special tooling, but also materials handling equipment. The removal of a wheel from a truck, and the tire from the wheel are best done using industrial tire changing equipment.

It is usually impossible for the expert to provide this type of equipment at the site. Arrangements should be made either with site personnel, or with outside contractors to provide the necessary goods and services on a timely basis.

It is essential that the needs be anticipated and arranged for by the expert. It is also essential that all the work of the personnel performing the operations be directed and supervised by the expert personally.

MOBILE EQUIPMENT

It is often necessary to make field measurements using equipment that is mobile, but not portable. Typical of these measurements are field radiography, large engine or motor mechanical output, high-voltage heavy-duty electrical power analysis, and real-time materials testing.

In these cases the mobile laboratory becomes a necessity. Most major population centers have commercial laboratories with appropriate mobile equipment. Here again, the expert has the duty to anticipate the need, make the arrangements, and supervise the work of the contractor.

PHOTOGRAPHIC EQUIPMENT

The still camera and the video camera are the "sine qua non" of accident investigation. Every investigating expert should become proficient, although not necessarily professional, in the use of this equipment. Since this gear is used both to document the visit as well as to prepare courtroom exhibits, it should be of high commercial quality.

Unless you are a professional photographer your primary camera should be a high quality thirty five millimeter single lens reflex camera capable of taking good close-up shots. My own preference is for a programmable camera with automatic and manual modes, and with manual focussing. If you don't want to be concerned with camera settings, completely automatic high-quality SLRs are readily available.

A basic system for the personal use of the investigator might be as follows.

1. 35 millimeter camera body, automatic and manual exposure, manual focus, Olympus OM2S or equal, or 35 millimeter camera body, automatic and manual exposure, automatic focus with manual override, Olympus iS1 or equal.

2. Lenses—50mm f1.8, 28mm f1.8, 75mm f 3.5, or 35–75mm f3.5 zoom lens. Do not use lens telephoto or wide angle adapters to avoid degradation of detail. Lens/camera combination should be capable of closeups to 18 inches or better for macro work and copying of labels and markings.

3. Automatic flash attachment if the camera body does not contain built in flash.

4. Light weight tripod for time exposure and investigator participation in the photo demonstration using self-timer.

5. Appropriate film. Kodacolor Gold 200 in a 24 exposure roll is recommended for most applications. The speed is adequate, the detail good, and the number of exposures appropriate for most assignments. Limiting a roll of film to a single assignment is appropriate even if only a few photographs are taken. For some assignments a higher film speed (400 to 1600) may be required.

Reliability through redundancy is a good procedure, particularly where it would be diffcult or impossible to rephotograph the site. I have used the redundancy technique myself ever since I took a series of pictures without the film being threaded properly in the camera. The resulting blank roll of film was a lesson learned.

Redundancy can be provided by a second camera or by a second photographer. As a backup camera I sometimes use a large format camera with a Polaroid back to assure that some usable photos are available before leaving the scene. I have also had good success using client investigative personnel to take backup photographs, and greater success using good commercial photographers.

Extreme closeup work and photomicrography is a job for experts with seismically stable photographic equipment. Radiography and thermography are also jobs for specialists if good quality exhibits are desired. Again, remember that unless the work is performed at your direction and under your supervision, you may not be allowed to testify as to its significance.

CINEMATOGRAPHY

The camcorder is the most effective new tool in the bag of the investigative expert. It can be used in two modes. It can be set up to document the entire investigation. Under these conditions the camera is set up for an overall view on a tripod, and allowed to run continuously.

Alternately, the camera can be used to document specific operations, static or dynamic, which can be used to refresh memory, or demonstrate technical points to lay personnel. Remember that under most conditions audio as well as video is being recorded. Remember also that the tapes in their entirety are usually available to the opposition.

There are three common formats available, VHS, VHS-C, and 8 millimeter. While the C and 8mm camcorders are usually smaller and handier to use, the VHS format produces a tape playable without conversion on a standard VCR.

The recommended selection is the smallest camcorder available using standard VHS cartridges, having at least an 8x power zoom, a low light capability of 2 lux, high speed shutter, macro focus, and editing functions. The Magnavox VHS camcorder CVM310AV is typical of a number of full size units meeting these specifications.

If portability is of utmost importance, the Sony CCD-FX411 8mm Handycam, or the Sharp VL-M6U are good alternatives, although conversion is necessary to use the 8mm tapes on a standard VCR.

Finally you should have duplicating and editing facilities for the tapes. Using the camcorder as an output unit, tapes can be copied on any high quality VCR having separate audio and video inputs. A good television set with monitor inputs, and a video enhancer completes the copy setup.

As with the still cameras, the ouput quality of the video system is critical to success. Get the best you can afford.

APPENDIX E

Legal Forms and Documents

The following sample legal documents are patterned after those currently used in the Florida State Court system. They are generic and similar to what will be found in the Federal Court system and in most other states. The reader who is familiar with these samples will have no problem translating their import and intent to comparable documents from other court systems.

These documents include:

1. Complaint

2. Subpoena Duces Tecum

3. Interrogatories

4. Request for Production

5. Subpoena for Trial

Note that in the interrogatories the answers are those of only one of the defendants. The other defendant is required to submit a separate set of answers.

IN THE CIRCUIT COURT, _____

JUDICIAL CIRCUIT, IN AND FOR

_____ COUNTY, FLORIDA

CASE NO.:

DIVISION:

JOHN DOE

       Plaintiff,

vs.

XYZ MANUFACTURING COMPANY,

a _____ corporation, and THE XYZ

DISTRIBUTORS, a Florida corporation,

       Defendants.

COMPLAINT

Plaintiff John Doe sues defendants and alleges:

1. This is an action for damages that exceed $10,000.

2.   At the time of the accident, plaintiff was a resident of _____ _____, _____ County, Florida.

3.   At all times material hereto, defendant XYZ Distributors, Inc. ("XYZ Dist."), was and is a Florida corporation with a principal place of business in _____ County, Florida.

4.   At all times material hereto, defendant XYZ Dist., Inc. was engaged in the business of selling and installing XYZ1000 model industrial robots of the type involved in this accident.

5.   At all times material hereto, defendant The XYZ Manufacturing Co.("XYZ") was engaged in the business of designing, manufacturing and selling XYZ industrial robots of the type that was involved in this accident.

6.   At all times material hereto, defendant XYZ Dist. engaged in solicitation or service activities within the State of Florida, and products, materials or things processed, serviced or manufactured by defendant XYZ Dist. were used within this state in the ordinary course of trade, commerce or use.

7.   At all times material hereto, defendant XYZ engaged in solicitation or service activities within the State of Florida, and products,

materials or things processed, serviced or manufactured by defendant XYZ were used within this state in the ordinary course of trade, commerce or use.

8.   On or about _____ plaintiff John Doe was employed by _____ Co. in _____ Florida.

9.   On or about _____ John Doe, in the course and scope of his employment, was operating an XYZ1000 industrial robot. He was operating the system in its normally intended manner.

10.   While plaintiff was using the machine for its intended purpose, the mechanism seized his arm causing the arm to be pulled down into a rolling machine pinch point.

11.   As a result, plaintiff John Doe was injured and he suffered resulting pain and suffering, disability, disfigurement, mental anguish, loss of capacity for the enjoyment of life, expense of hospitalization, medical and nursing care and treatment, loss of earnings, and loss of ability to earn money. The losses are permanent and plaintiff will suffer the losses in the future.

COUNT I

12.   Plaintiff John Doe realleges and incorporates the allegations of paragraphs 1 through 11 in this count as if fully set forth herein.

13. At all times, defendant XYZ Dist. knew or should have known that operators of the industrial robot system would use the equipment in the manner used by Mr. Doe.

14. The accident in question and plaintiff John Doe's injuries were proximately caused or contributed to by defects in the industrial robot system, all of which existed at the time the system left the control of defendant XYZ Dist., and all of which rendered the system unreasonably dangerous for its intended and reasonably foreseeable uses:

(a) The industrial robot system as designed, manufactured, sold and installed created an unreasonable risk of injury to an operator attempting to operate the equipment.

(b) The industrial robot system as designed, manufactured, sold and installed, was inadequate in that it could seize and harm the operator without warning.

(c) The robot should have been designed as a fail safe mechanism which would not operate if the operator was in danger.

(d) The operator should have been provided with a hand-held kill switch to stop the mechanism at any sign of danger

15. These defects caused or contributed to causing the accident in question and the injuries to plaintiff John Doe.

WHEREFORE, plaintiff demands judgment for damages against defendant XYZ Dist.

COUNT II

16.   Plaintiff John Doe realleges and incorporates the allegations of paragraphs 1 through 15 in this count as if fully set forth herein.

17.   At all times, defendant XYZ knew or should have known that operators of the industrial robot system would be required to use the equipment as used by John Doe.

18.   The accident in question and plaintiff John Doe's injuries were proximately caused or contributed to by defects in the industrial robot system, all of which existed at the time the mechanism left the control of defendant XYZ, and all of which rendered the mechanism unreasonably dangerous for its intended and reasonably foreseeable uses.

The defects of paragraph 14 a. to c. are repeated here

19.   These defects caused or contributed to causing the accident in question and the injuries to plaintiff John Doe.

WHEREFORE, plaintiff demands judgment for damages against defendant XYZ.

COUNT III

Plaintiff John Doe realleges and incorporates the allegations of paragraphs 1 through 19 in this count as if fully set forth herein.

20.   At all times, defendant XYZ Dist. knew or should have known that operators of the industrial robot system would be required to use the system in the manner used by John Doe,

21.   In selling and installing the industrial robot system, defendant XYZ Dist. had a duty to use reasonable care to afford protection to persons such as plaintiff John Doe who would foreseeably be using the system: but defendant XYZ Dist. breached that duty, in that as sold and installed by defendant XYZ Dist. the industrial robot system was unreasonably dangerous in the following respects:

(a)   The industrial robot system as designed, manufactured, sold and installed created an unreasonable risk of injury to an operator using the system.

(b)   The industrial robot system, as designed, manufactured, sold and installed, was inadequate in that it failed to stop operating immediately when the unit malfunctioned.

(c)   The system should have been designed with an emergency stop switch held by the operator.

(d)   Defendant XYZ Dist. failed to warn users, or warn users adequately, of the danger of using the mechanism if it failed to function properly.

(e)   Defendant XYZ Dist. failed to give adequate consideration to safety in the design, manufacture, sale and installation of the industrial robot system, including without limitation the failure to conduct safety tests, to have an adequate quality control system, to conduct adequate safety inspections and to have an appropriate system for receiving and responding to reports of injury.

22.   Such negligence caused or contributed to causing the accident in question and the injuries to plaintiff John Doe.

WHEREFORE, plaintiff demands judgment for damages against defendant XYZ Dist.

COUNT IV

Plaintiff John Doe realleges and incorporates the allegations of paragraphs 1 through 22 in this count as if fully set forth herein.

23.   At all times, defendant XYZ knew or should have known that operators of the industrial robot system would be required to use the system in the manner used by John Doe.

24. In designing, manufacturing and selling the robot systems, defendant XYZ had a duty to use reasonable care to afford protection to persons such as John Doe who would foreseeably be operating the mechanism; but defendant XYZ breached that duty, in that as designed, manufactured and sold by defendant XYZ the machine was unreasonably dangerous in the following respects:

The alleged defects of 21 a. to c. are repeated here.

(d) Defendant XYZ failed to warn users, or warn users adequately, of the danger of using the industrial robot system if the system failed to function properly.

(f) Defendant XYZ failed to give adequate consideration to safety in the design, manufacture, sale and installation of the industrial robot system, including without limitation the failure to conduct safety tests, to have an adequate quality control system, to conduct adequate safety inspections and to have an appropriate system for receiving and responding to reports of injury.

25. Such negligence caused or contributed to causing the accident in question and the injuries to plaintiff John Doe.

WHEREFORE, plaintiff demands judgment for damages against defendant XYZ.

DEMAND FOR JURY TRIAL

Plaintiff demands trial by jury.

Smith, Smith, Smith & Jones

_____
John Jones
Florida Bar I.D. No. xxxxxx

Attorneys for Plaintiff

IN THE CIRCUIT COURT, _____
JUDICIAL CIRCUIT, IN AND FOR
_____ COUNTY, FLORIDA.

CASE NO:
DIVISION:

John Doe

        Plaintiff,

vs.

XYZ Manufacturing Co., a _____ corporation,

        Defendant.

SUBPOENA DUCES TECUM FOR DEPOSITION

THE STATE OF FLORIDA:

TO: JAMES X. PERT
     Street Address
     City, State, Zip Code

YOU ARE COMMANDED to appear before a person authorized by law to take depositions, at 10:00 a.m., on _____, _____ 2, 1999, at _____ for the taking of your deposition in this action and to have with you at that time and place those items and things as listed on Exhibit "A" attached hereto.

If you fail to appear, you may be in contempt of Court.

You are subpoenaed to appear by the following attorneys and unless excused from this subpoena by these attorneys or the Court, you shall respond to this subpoena as directed.

_____
(Court Seal)

As Clerk of said Court

By: _____

               As Deputy Clerk

WILLIAMS & WILLIAMS, P.A.
WM. WILLIAMS
1234 Main Street
Anytown, USA

EXHIBIT "A"

1. Any and all reports (preliminary, final or otherwise), rough drafts, work sheets and materials in any manner connected with the opinions or conclusions reached concerning the subject matter of your expert opinion;

2. Any and all materials considered, consulted and used by you as a basis or predicate for your opinions and conclusions, including, but not limited to, published reports by any private or governmental agency, text books, articles, data or other documents furnished by the party engaging your services;

3. All computations, calculations, formulas considered, utilized, produced or in any manner connected with your opinions or conclusions;

4. Any and all written instructions, including, but not limited to, correspondence, memoranda, notes, photographs including any provided to you or taken by you or at your direction, and any and all other materials provided to you by the persons and/or entities and representatives thereof employing you in this case;

5. Any and all documents reflecting time spent and effort expended by you in preparation for, and consideration of the opinion(s) with regard to this case, including but not limited to, time records, billing statements, calendars and appointment books;

6. All scientific, technical or professional texts, journals, articles, or other writings authored by you, in whole or in part, pertaining to, in whole or in part, which in any way may relate to your opinion(s) regarding this case;

7. The results of any and all tests you have performed, or that have been performed at your direction concerning the accident in question;

8. A current curriculum vitae.

IN THE CIRCUIT COURT, _____
JUDICIAL CIRCUIT, IN AND FOR
_____ COUNTY, FLORIDA

CASE NO.:

DIVISION:

JOHN DOE

Plaintiff,

vs.

XYZ MANUFACTURING CO., A _____
corporation, and XYZ Distributors,
a Florida corporation,

Defendants.

PLAINTIFF'S FIRST SET OF INTERROGATORIES TO DEFENDANT XYZ DISTRIBUTORS, INC.

Pursuant to Rule 1.340, Florida Rules of Civil Procedure, the defendant XYZ Distributors, Inc. is requested and required to answer the following interrogatories propounded by the plaintiff John Doe under oath and in writing, within the time and manner prescribed by law:

1. What is your name, address and, if you are answering for someone else, your official position?

Henry Wilson, President
XYZ Distributors, Inc.

2.   Is your company name correctly stated in the style of the complaint? If not, what is the correct corporate name?

Yes

3.   Describe in detail, each act or omission on the part of plaintiff you contend constituted negligence that was a contributing legal cause of the accident in question.

Plaintiff himself was negligent in failing to pay attention to operating machinery. Ongoing investigation.

4.   List the names and addresses of all persons believed or known by you, your agents or attorneys to have any knowledge concerning any of the issues raised by the pleadings and specify the subject matter about which the witness has knowledge.

Unknown at this time.

5.   List the name, residence address, business address and telephone number of each person believed or known by you, your agents or attorneys to have heard or who is purported to have heard the plaintiff make any statement, remark or comment concerning the accident described in the complaint and the substance of each statement, remark or comment.

Same as answer 4.

6.   Regarding the industrial robot and the rolling mill which were involved in the accident (hereafter "the products"), please state:

(a)   Who manufactured said products?
(b)   When the manufacture of the particular products was completed.
(c)   When would the products have left your control?
(d)   To whom were they shipped?
(e)   What instructional brochures, warranty cards, and operational manuals, would have accompanied the products when they left your possession?

Object to lumping robot and mill together. We have no knowledge of the mill. The robot was manufactured by an entity other than XYZ Distributors, presumably XYZ Manufacturing Co. We do not know when the manufacture was completed. Other data is being developed.

7. Did any company other than the defendant company manufacture or fabricate any part of the products involved in this case? If so, please give the parts in question manufactured or fabricated by a party other than the defendant.

Unknown.

8. Since the prototype has been completed, have there been any changes in the design or configuration of the products that would affect the way the robot functions when parts fail? Give the reason for the change, the date of the change, and who was responsible.

Unknown.

9. Are there any committees or groups within the corporation primarily concerned with the safety of the consumer, either as to design, modification, warnings, advertising, or operating instructions? If so, please provide:

    (a) The name or names of the groups or committees.
    (b) The names and titles of all members in the group for the past five years.
    (c) The name of the person or persons who kept the minutes of the meetings for the past 5 years and where said minutes are stored.

There are no groups concerned solely with safety. Rather, all employees view consumer safety as a primary concern in the sale of its products.

10. Are there any other groups or committees, although not primarily concerned with the safety of the consumer, but nonetheless concerned with the safety of the consumer? If so, please state:

    (a) The names of any such committee or group.
    (b) The names and titles of all members in the group for the past 5 years.

(c)   Whether minutes of any meetings are kept in regard to the group's activity, and if so, where said minutes are stored or retained.

See answer 9.

11.   What is the name and model description of the products in question?

Model XYZ1000 Industrial Robot.

12.   Have any lawsuits been brought against the defendant where it is alleged that the same or a similar product resulted in any personal injury or death? If so, please state the name and address of the claimant, claimant's attorney, and the basic nature of the claim, whether it is a property damage claim, a personal injury claim or a death claim.

Not to my knowledge

13.   Is the defendant aware of any prior claim that either has been settled or did not result in suit, or that are pending and not in suit? If so, please give the name and address of the claimant (or claimant's attorney) and the date of the claim.

Objection: overbroad, vague, burdensome and irrelevant. Notwithstanding this objection, this Defendant is not aware of any prior claims against it where it is alleged that the same or a similar product caused injury or death.

14.   Does the defendant corporation attempt to analyze or categorize warranty claims in any way? If so, please describe in detail the manner in which warranty claims are categorized or analyzed.

Yes. Warranty claims are filed by the type of part that needs repair or replacement.

15.   Did you have liability insurance coverage that protects you from the damages sought by the complaint? If so:

(a)   What is the name of the insurance company having the coverage?

(b)   What is the extent of coverage provided in the policy or policies of insurance, including coverage for both personal injury and property damage?

(c)   What is the policy number of each policy?

(d)   Is there any deductible or retained self insurance? If so, the amount.

(e)   Is coverage afforded for all counts in the complaint, including punitive damages, if any?

(f)   In what year did the defendant first obtain insurance from said companies?

See attached list.

16.   Have any insurance companies ever made recommendations in writing as to the safety of the type of products in question? If so, the date of said writing, and the person signing said writing.

Not to my knowledge.

17.   Do you intend to call any nonmedical expert witnesses at the trial of this case?

If so, please state:

(a)   Identify each witness;

(b)   Describe his qualifications as an expert;

(c)   State the subject matter upon which he is expected to testify;

(d)   State the substance of the facts and opinions to which he is expected to testify; and

(e)   Give a summary of the grounds for each opinion.

Undetermined at this time.

18.   If you, your attorneys or other representative have custody or control of the original of a copy of any written statement relative to the issues of this case, please state:

(a)   The name and address of each person giving such statement;

(b)   The date on which each statement was given;

(c)   The place where each statement was given;

(d)   Whether or not such statement is or was signed by the person making such statement;

(e)   The name, address and employer of the person taking each such statement;

(f)   The name, address and employer of each person who witnessed the taking of such statement; and

(g)   Whether or not a copy of such statement was given to the person who made the subject statement.

Objection: work product.

19.   If you, your attorneys or other representatives have interviewed or contacted any party or lay witness with regard to the issues of this case, other than those persons listed in the answer to the preceding interrogatory, please state:

(a)   The name and address of the person so interviewed or contacted.

(b)   The name, address and employer of the person who interviewed or contacted such person.

(c)   The date and place of each such interview or contact.

(d)   Whether such interview or contact was by telephone, in person, or otherwise.

(e)   Whether or not such interview was recorded in any manner, and if your answer is in the affirmative, please describe the manner of recordation and state whether or not the person interviewed or contacted was advised that the interview or contact was recorded.

Objection: overly broad; work product privilege.

20.   If any model, map or drawing which in any way relates to the issues of this case is in your custody or subject to the control of you, your attorneys or representatives, please state:

(a)   The name and address of the person who designed, prepared or constructed each such model, map or drawing.

(b)   The general subject of each such model, map or drawing.

(c)   The number of models, maps or drawings so designed, prepared or constructed.

(d)   The name and address of the present custodian of each such model, map or drawing.

None.

21.   Describe specifically all facts, reports, photographs, statements, theories or other information upon which defendant bases its affirmative defenses.

Objection: vague, overly broad, work product privilege.

22.   Since the products referred to above left the control of defendant, have there been any changes in their condition? If so, describe changes in detail.

Unknown.

CERTIFICATE OF SERVICE

I HEREBY CERTIFY that the original and one copy of the foregoing interrogatories have been furnished to the process server to be served on defendant XYZ Distributors, Inc. and _____, its Registered Agent, at _____, Florida this ____ day of _____, 1999.

Smith, Smith, Smith & Jones, P.A.

_____
John Jones
Florida Bar No. _____
Street Address
City, State, Zip Code
Telephone Number
Attorneys for Plaintiff

STATE OF   )
) ss.
COUNTY OF   )

      Before me, the undersigned authority, personally appeared, _____

_____, who being first duly sworn,

depose(s) and say(s):

      That _____ is/are the person(s) named in the fore-

going interrogatories, that _____ has/have read the same,

know(s) the contents thereof and that the same are true.

      _____

Sworn to and subscribed before me
this ____ day of _____, 1999.

_____
Notary Public, State and County
Aforesaid

My Commission Expires:

      I HEREBY CERTIFY that the original answers to the foregoing
interrogatories have been furnished to: John Jones, Esquire, attorney for
plaintiff, (address) Florida, by _____ this _____
day of _____, 1999.

      _____
        Attorney

IN THE CIRCUIT COURT, _____
JUDICIAL CIRCUIT, IN AND FOR
_____ COUNTY, FLORIDA

CASE NO.:

DIVISION:

JOHN DOE

       Plaintiff,

vs.

XYZ DISTRIBUTORS, INC. a Florida
corporation, and THE XYZ MANUFACTURING
CO., a _____ corporation,

       Defendants.

___

PLAINTIFF'S REQUEST TO PRODUCE TO DEFENDANTS XYZ DISTRIBUTORS, INC. AND XYZ MANUFACTURING CO.

Pursuant to the applicable Florida Rules of Civil Procedure, plaintiff, by and through his undersigned attorney, requests defendants XYZ Distributors, Inc. and XYZ Manufacturing Co. to produce and to permit plaintiff to inspect and to copy each of the following documents:

1. Any and all installation, maintenance, parts and operator's instructions relating to the industrial robot system, as well as all its components, parts and operational systems attached thereto, which were installed as referred to in the Complaint, including but not limited

to the pneumatic and/or hydraulic apparatus, electrical system, electrical controls, piping diagrams, wiring diagrams and safety features.

2. Any and all installation, instructions, manuals and any other written materials prepared by defendant XYZ Manufacturing Co. and/or furnished to defendant XYZ Distributors, Inc. regarding the industrial robot system and any of the components or systems described above.

3. Any and all written warranties for the subject industrial robot system.

4. Any and all brochures, booklets or other promotional materials featuring the subject industrial robot system.

5. Any and all bills, invoices, purchase orders, bills of lading or other documents showing evidence of the sale and delivery of the industrial robot system in question to its original purchasers and if applicable, all subsequent purchasers or owners.

6. Any and all specifications, blueprints and design drawings regarding the subject industrial robot system.

7. Any and all instructions and warnings on the industrial robot system and copies of all documents distributed with the subject industrial robot system.

8.   Photographs of the industrial robot system.

9.   Any and all letters of warning, recall notices or the like sent out by you regarding the subject industrial robot system at any time whatsoever.

10.   Any and all citations or other notices from governmental or quasi-governmental entities relating to problems or dangers with the type of industrial robot system discussed in the Complaint.

11.   A descriptive narrative and other details regarding safety attachments, appliances and other safety features on or available for the industrial robot system.

12.   Copies of all correspondence or other documents between defendants relating to the industrial robot system prior to the subject incident.

13.   Copies of all correspondence or other documents between defendants relating to the industrial robot system subsequent to the subject incident.

14.   All governmental or industry standards relating to the design, manufacture and operation of the industrial robot system.

15.   Copies of all incident reports and notifications to defendants relating to incidents involving injuries to persons caused or alleged to

be caused by industrial robot systems of the same or similar design specification to the subject system, which occurred prior to the subject incident.

16. Copies of all incident reports and notifications to defendants relating to incidents involving injuries to persons caused by industrial robot systems having the same or similar design specification to the subject system, which occurred subsequent to the subject incident.

17. Copies of all incident reports and notifications to defendants relating to the injury suffered by plaintiff John Doe in the incident which is the subject of the above-captioned lawsuit.

18. Photographs indicating any changes in the design of the subject industrial robot system which have been made at any time whatsoever.

19. Copies of all inspections and maintenance reports for the subject industrial robot system.

20. Copies of the complaints in all lawsuits filed against defendants claiming personal injuries as the result of the use of the industrial robot systems of the same or similar design specifications to the subject system.

SMITH, SMITH, SMITH & JONES, P.A.

_____

John Jones
Florida Bar I.D. No. _____
Street Address
City, State, Zip Code
Telephone No.

Attorneys for Plaintiff

IN THE CIRCUIT COURT, _____
JUDICIAL CIRCUIT, IN AND FOR
_____ COUNTY, FLORIDA.

CASE NO.:
DIVISION:

JOHN DOE

Plaintiff,

vs.

XYZ MANUFACTURING COMPANY, a _____
corporation; and XYZ DISTRIBUTORS, INC.
a Florida corporation,

Defendants.

SUBPOENA FOR TRIAL

THE STATE OF FLORIDA:

TO: JAMES X. PERT
Street Address
City, State, Zip Code

YOU ARE COMMANDED to appear before the Honorable ____
_____, Judge of the Court, at the _____ County Courthouse,
(Street Address), (City), Florida, at 9:00 a.m. on _____, 1999,
or as soon thereafter as this matter may be heard, to testify at the trial
of this action.

If you fail to appear, you may be in contempt of Court.

You are subpoenaed to appear by the following attorney and unless excused from this subpoena by this attorney of the Court, you shall
respond to this subpoena as directed.

WITNESS my hand and the seal of this Court, this ____ day of
_____ 1999.

                                          _____

As Clerk of said Court

(Court Seal)

By: _____
As Deputy Clerk

John Jones
Attorney for Plaintiff

INDEX